CTRL ALT REPEAT

A FAMILY'S STRUGGLE TO RECLAIM LIFE HACKED BY OCD

DR. SUNIL PUNJABI

Dedicated to my lovely wife, Sonal, who has to go through the struggles everyday but does not lose hope.

Dedicated also to my wonderful son, Shlok, who didn't ask for this and yet showed more maturity many times than I did.

Contents

Contents

The Beginning

CHAPTER I

Preface

This is not your usual fairy tale that begins with '*once upon a time*' and ends with '*and they lived happily ever after*'. In fact, this is not a fairly tale at all. This is a story of my family's fight with obsessive-compulsive disorder, OCD for short. OCD, for those who do not know, is not an adjective. One cannot say, 'I'm so OCD that I like clean desks' Saying that is similar to saying, 'I'm so cancer that...', or 'I'm so brain tumor that....' Using the term OCD flippantly amounts to trivializing the pain of a sufferer and the sufferer's family. OCD is a severely debilitating mental disorder that can strike anyone at any time. Perfunctory research will reveal just how common it is and how devastating it can be. Through this book, you will get a glimpse of what goes on behind closed doors in a family where one member is affected by OCD.

Research says roughly 2-3 percent of the people have or will develop some form of OCD. That is 1 out of every 30 people. So, if you have 500 followers on Instagram or Facebook, roughly 15 of them could have OCD. OCD can attack kids, grownups, old people, men, women alike. To our misfortune, it struck my wife of eleven years, Sonal. It brought out the worst in her since she was under its complete control. That brought out the worst in me because I could see excesses on the part of Sonal that I could not understand and could not deal with maturely.

Sonal's OCD was tenacious, unbeatable, indefatigable. No adjective can do justice to describe the disorder effectively. We have been having a tug o' war with it for many years now, and for the better part of the game, it has been winning. We have been relentlessly fighting it together, egging each other on, sometimes losing hope, at other times springing back into action. Our peace of mind, happiness, the joys of connubial bliss, the joys of parenthood – all expropriated, all sacrificed at the altar of the disorder. We continue to slog in our efforts to wrest back the control from the OCD monster (as Sonal sees it), which we hope to achieve someday. This story is about our travails.

CHAPTER II

The Diwali Fiasco

As I was driving to Bandra, where we had been invited for a Diwali dinner by my wife's cousin, Sonal (my wife of seven years) sitting in shock behind and Shlok, the five-year-old apple of my eye, sitting confused and scared with me in the front, my own mind was awhirl with a million thoughts like raging impulses across agitated synapses. A cocktail of unwanted emotions was searing through me like sharp, tiny bullets, boring holes wherever they made contact. Horror – upon seeing my wife bested by such insignificance. Confusion – at the apparent absurdity of it all. Apprehension – would the fabric that held us together start crumbling? Consternation and self-reproach – for not having noticed it so far. Concern – for Shlok's well-being and sanity. Anger – at Sonal for not understanding what I was trying to tell her and instead arguing with me. Anger – also at myself for supposedly being the head of the family and not dealing with this situation deftly. Much as I tried to architect my thoughts into a coherent, understandable structure, they insisted on entirely being edgeless clouds of inchoate matter – ill-formed, stunted and warped.

I still couldn't believe it. Two ants! Two ants? I was scarcely paying attention to the radio churning out old melodies of Kishore Kumar and Mohammed Rafi on the car stereo of my black Honda City, which otherwise I would have been singing along. Even Sonal and Shlok were terrifyingly silent. All I wanted to do was to have the evening end soon and it hadn't even begun. Two ants! I shook my head in disbelief.

Just to make sense of the bizarre spectacle that I had been a witness to, a few minutes earlier, I ran the scene through my mind again for the umpteenth time to make yet another futile attempt at understanding what exactly happened. It was the third day of Diwali of 2009. Every year, for the last seven years, we had been dining *chez* one of Sonal's relatives on this day. It was a ritual that came with the territory of being married to a girl with a huge extended family. Sonal has no fewer than ten uncles and aunts and twenty-five cousins. They have more than 'cordial relations' with each of them. This family is a strong case for 'rishta nibhaana' (maintain relationships willingly), as against 'kaam chalaana' (get by with the minimum). That year too, we had been invited over by one of Sonal's cousins.

They lived in Bandra and to reach there from our apartment, in Andheri, we had to leave at least 75-90 minutes earlier. We would have to weave our way through the Juhu traffic, drive by the Juhu seaside, cross the Santa Cruz Police Station and Linking Road and then reach Hill Road in Bandra. Knowing how things were likely to get delayed, I had impressed upon Sonal, the need to leave at 6.30 PM to arrive at the latest by 8 PM.

During the daytime, time seemed to be passing languorously, just the way I like it during the holidays. Still, towards evening, it already seemed like we would be late. Since Diwali is in winter, it was also getting dark outside. Lately, I had come upon the realization that this was becoming a kind of pattern. We were to leave in less than an hour, and Sonal still wasn't in any state of readiness to go. She isn't the type to take too long deciding on what clothes to wear, what accessories to pair with them, how much makeup to apply, unlike the stereotypes women are cast in. That wasn't the reason for the delay.

But I truly wish that she was that stereotypical woman and that was the real reason for the delay, instead of what the reality was. Lately, our delays were caused by an annoying habit that she had developed. She had gotten into the irksome routine of wanting to maintain extreme cleanliness of the apartment. I make it sound like a bad thing because this fetish was bordering on the excessive. Whom am I kidding? On the other side of excessive, it was far away from the centre. Freakish is more like it.

Whatever time of the day it was, the apartment needed to be spic and span. Clean as the proverbial whistle! Whenever we had to go somewhere, she would leave the apartment only when she was one hundred percent satisfied with the cleanliness and tidiness of the place. She wanted everything to be prim and proper, everything in its rightful place. It was not uncommon to see her dressed at her finest, make-up et al., and still have a dusting cloth in her hand for some last-minute cleaning. Even seconds before leaving, she would wipe invisible dirt off a surface or two with the dusting cloth and subject it to a particular forensic-ish scrutiny. I would idly imagine her walking all around with a magnifying glass in her hand, inspecting the apartment for some missed spot. I would even make fun of her and tell her I would buy her one. She would give me one of her dazzling smiles and let it pass.

Sonal would start from the bedroom at the far end of the apartment, a rub-a-dub here and a rub-a-dub there. From there, she would move to the kitchen and repeat. Then, onto the living-room and repeat, like a tireless soldier, decimating enemies, thoroughly and systematically. Only then would we leave the house. This would almost always be done long after we ought to have already left for wherever we were supposed to go, and it would irk me. I like reaching wherever I go on time, and I make an effort to be punctual. Here, despite the delay, Sonal would waste more time in her crusade while Shlok and I would be ready and waiting.

On this day, too, as usual, fifteen minutes after it was time for us to leave, Shlok and I at the ready, he in a smart Indian ethnic *chudidar-kurta*, neatly combed (and oiled – he didn't know enough to object to his hair being oiled and Sonal took full advantage of the situation by applying obscene amounts of oil on his scalp, as often as she could) hair, talcum powdered face, smelling of jasmine and wearing cute looking black sandals in his small feet and me in my usual checked shirt and blue jeans with Lee Cooper shoes, and a measured application of Brut deodorant. Feeling dapper but twiddling thumbs. Waiting. For Sonal to finish her cleaning. Sitting on the sofa, watching random programmes on TV. Flicking channels without registering what was playing, and inwardly fuming while Sonal was making sure the apartment was cleaner than ever. Occasionally casting frustrated glances at Sonal, who looked resplendent in an off-white *salwar kameez* with a golden-ish *dupatta*). She had on bangles that adorned her right hand, a sleek watch that adorned the left, lipstick that she liked and kohl that I liked. Beautiful!

The only thing that marred the scene was the cloth in her hand. The bedroom was inspected first, and with some fuss, it passed muster, after a scrub here and a dab there. The kitchen also made it. Like an army major inspecting a file of soldiers and pulling them up for their misses. I could imagine each room heaving a sigh of relief as Sonal was done with them. Finally, when she reached the drawing-room, my hopes of a speedy departure rose, and so did my spirits.

The *Lakshmi* idol and the *pooja thali* were kept on the centre table, which was ironically, against the wall. Sonal was cleaning that up. She removed the ash of the *agarbattis* and *dhoops* that had run their courses and lit new ones in their place. She replenished the oil in the oil lamps for them to keep being lit for a while longer. Then she cleaned the dining table and set the box of sweets in a container kept in a vessel filled with water so that no ants could reach the sweets.

Just as she was finishing up, and I was finally cooling down after having simmered all this while at Sonal for having delayed our departure, the event that would be the seminal point in our lives made its horrific presence felt. While Sonal was wiping the dining table around the box of sweets, she came face to face with her nemesis. It is funny to call them a nemesis because it isn't lizards or cockroaches that we are talking about, which most women (or even men) are scared of. It was two ants. Two ants! Bam! It was as if we were hit by a tornado. Things went in a complete whirl from that point. Sonal was utterly overwhelmed with fear, horror writ large on her face. White! Shaking! After going through multiple contortions of face and mind, trying hard to control her fear, when she couldn't, she finally burst into tears. Downright howling. Uncontrollably. Her kohl mixed with her tears and made dark blotches on her face, ruining her princess-ly looks. A torrent of tears streaming down her face, nose running, trying to keep up with the tears and nearly succeeding.

At that instant, Sonal forgot everything else. She forgot that we were to go out. She forgot that she had taken pains to get ready. She forgot that we were waiting. She forgot that we existed at all. All she wanted to do was to lay her hands on a fresh dusting cloth again, wipe-wipe-wipe to get those ants off the table, out of the drawing-room, and out of the apartment. She wanted to make sure that there were no more ants left, no matter how much time and effort that took. She pulled out one of her clean dusting cloths, of which we had dozens at home at any point, went into the bathroom and washed it with generous amounts of soap and water (even new ones needed to be broken in with a thorough scrub with soap and water before she would consider them worthy of making contact with any surface in the apartment).

Then she spent a full twenty minutes cleaning the table up; wiping the entire surface multiple times, checking and rechecking to see if there were any more ants left that needed to be taken care of or if there was any sweet spilled on the table that would need cleaning up.

Her crying, even as she cleaned, had not abated. That continued with full gusto. She cursed her stars and God and me and everything and everyone else she could think of for the ants in the apartment. She ranted about disastrous scenarios that her hyper-zealous mind painted for her, about there being more ants in the apartment than she could take care of, about having lost the battle of cleanliness and about her wish to die.

A chill crawled down my spine slowly and continuously in small but unmistakable bursts at the sight of this bizarre spectacle. Years back, while on the phone, I had absent-mindedly clicked on an icon on my computer, which said 'Smile'. That was when small game apps were forwarded through emails by friends and I had downloaded it to my desktop. When I double-clicked on the icon, it activated a message saying, '*All the files will be deleted from your computer.*'

I frantically searched for a cancel button and hit the escape key multiple times to stop the operation. To no avail. The screen showed all my files getting deleted.

'*Oh, my god*', I thought, '*I have clicked on a virus.*' I was dumbstruck. For a couple of seconds, I blanked out. I couldn't even hear what the person on the phone was saying. I thought I could have a stroke. Turns out, it was an anti-virus software advertisement and my files were not really deleted. What a cruel, cruel joke! But those few moments were like my life turning upside down. That is how I was feeling at that moment. Sadly, this wasn't a warning app or an ad. It was happening in front of me. Live! In real time!

I fluttered about helplessly and uselessly, hoping that she would calm down. I tried to make soothing noises to ease her discomfort, which were summarily spurned by her. I went to hold her, but she pushed me away because I was standing in the way. This was the first of many times that I have felt like a used condom. Utterly useless.

Shlok had, in the meantime, also begun to cry because he was scared to see his mother cry and couldn't understand why his mother was crying, just a little kid, as he was. Hell, forget him, even I couldn't understand why my wife was crying. What was it about the ants that caused such abject terror for Sonal? I was utterly at bay for a possible explanation to this grotesque scene, which I had suddenly been forced to become a part of. But I mindfully had to remind myself that I was also ostensibly the man of the house. Supposedly, in charge. I didn't have an elder in the house to go to and seek comfort or ask for a solution. I had to handle the situation myself. I had to somehow first calm my jittery nerves down.

Then I had to soothe Sonal's anxiety. I had to get her to a level where she could deal with her fear, at least temporarily. I had to remind her that we had an appointment and that we were expected there right now. I had to get her to wash and make her face up again. I had to convince her that it was alright to stop worrying about the ants and that there weren't any more of them in the apartment right then. We could tackle the menace on a more permanent basis when we returned. I had to get her to leave for dinner with us, even if to distract her from the scene and the horror that it represented. I had to comfort Shlok and lie to him that everything was fine, lest it torment his tiny, five year-old brain too much. I had to get us to try and enjoy the dinner. So, the dutiful husband and father that I believe I was, I did my best. After several pleas and entreaties, we exited the apartment *en route* to our dinner date. Throughout the journey, there was pin-drop silence in the car. All of us were going over the macabre spectacle in our minds over and over again. Wondering when this horrific game had begun and if it could have been played differently.

While going over the events of the recent past, it dawned on me that Sonal, my wife of seven years, the nucleus of my microcosmic family, who had hitherto been an average girl with her share of strengths and weaknesses, had developed a less than average quirk. It was a mortal fear of ants. A series of instances crossed my mind when I noticed this strange aversion – for aversion is what I thought it was, and I had seen enough instances of that in the past. Either I was too dumb or she, too sneaky because the extent of her fear was unknown to me, even if its existence was.

That we reached our destination late was inevitable and totally irrelevant. That we had to lie through our teeth to explain our delay (we sure as hell weren't going to be honest about it) was beside the point. Somehow we scraped through the evening with part bravado, part denial. But an abundance of questions plagued my mind throughout. How badly the incident had affected Sonal was alarming. When had the aversion metamorphosed into a phobia as severe as this? Why had I been so blind, nay, so dumb to not be able to see it? What were we to do? What was happening to my wife? What would happen to our lives? How would Shlok be able to take it? I am adept at putting up a brave face in times of adversity, and I did so here as well, but despite my shallow, phony bravado, I was trembling inwardly.

After that first *tete-a-tete* with this truckload of panic caused by two insignificant ants, I knew. Without a shadow of doubt, I knew that Sonal was not merely averse to ants as I had been thinking (or hoping for?) I knew that she was not just fastidious about her cleaning routine. I knew that it was no ordinary fixation. It hit me hard to admit to myself that she was mentally unwell. Seriously, mentally unwell. This was well beyond our amateurish (read negligible) capabilities to handle. Or even understand. I knew that she needed nothing less than professional help to come out of this. I knew that she needed it fast. Yes, I knew.

CHAPTER III

The New Apartment

"'Every moment is a fresh beginning.' - T. S. Eliot"

In addition to every other aversion that she had, Sonal has always had an aversion to ants as well. Our apartment, which was my parents' house, where Sonal and I stayed for the first few years (from 2003 to 2005) after I got married, had always had a lot of ants. There would be ants in the kitchen, ants in the few potted plants and ants in the bathroom. Ants on the clothes' rods, ants in the cupboard. One line of ants would always be visible somewhere or the other. They are still visible there. They mind their own business, and my parents mind theirs. It doesn't bother my parents now, and it didn't bother them (or me), then. But it bothered Sonal. Greatly. No matter how hard she labored with it, they would just not go away. If one thing can be said about ants, it could very well be tenacity. She would clean a line of ants one day, and they would reappear the following day. We plugged whatever holes we could see with soap (which is supposed to keep ants away), but the ants would find some other crevice to crop out of.

It was almost funny the way Sonal and the ants would engage in a fight to the finish. The problem (her aversion) was not so severe initially. It seemed like a normal aversion to creepy crawlies, so it didn't concern any of us too much. It was, in fact, amusing to see her being so fastidious about cleanliness and actually endeared her to me. I thought she was so hygiene conscious. Structured and organized. A place for everything and everything in its place. The proverbial 'not-a-strand-out-of-place' kind of girl.

None of us really read too much into her aversion for ants. Big mistake. I often wish I had had the foresight to isolate her aversion to ants from her other fears and deal with it while it was still manageable. But I didn't. This led to her condition going from bad to worse. Also, I keep asking myself in retrospect: where does one draw a line? When does one decide that a particular aversion is crossing the line? Would things have been any different if we had known earlier? I don't know. If I were given to melodrama, I would hold a grudge against myself for that. But that is water under the bridge now.

When Sonal got pregnant, the hitherto aversion (at least in our minds) became a need to keep the house clean and ant-free for her child. She didn't want to bring up her child in a house with so many ants for fear that they would bite the child. I also, didn't fancy my child being bitten by ants, but this was a bit much. I suspect a small story that she had heard would have been responsible for that, though Sonal doesn't seem to remember it now. Apparently, in some house there were ants and a small baby. One day when the baby was sleeping, a few ants entered the baby's ear and caused an infection that led to the baby's death. I remember this story being narrated, but I don't know if it is a true story or a figment of someone's fertile but morbid imagination. I repeat I think that was the reason why Sonal was so averse to having ants (and no other insect) at home. She doesn't remember it and she denies that that was the reason.

Whatever it was, a lot of cleaning had begun at home. After Shlok was born, her efforts to keep the apartment ant-free raised manifold. Sonal started ensuring that at least the room that we occupied was as ant-free as possible. She would dust the windows and other furniture, and she would check and cross-check for ants in the clothes too. One day, to our misfortune, she did find an ant in Shlok's diaper that had bitten him and made him cry. She was immensely sad and ended up self-castigating for hours on end. That led to her needing to keep the room clean to the point of obsession, and she would spend about an hour everyday cleaning up a single room. She would wake up in the morning, and after a cup of tea, without which her day does not start, her cleaning routine would begin.

While others would finish whatever little dusting was required and done in the rest of the household, even though they would start it later, Sonal would still be at it. Meticulously wiping every nook and cranny of the room, keeping an eye out for ants, and quite literally drowning them with insecticide spray if she saw any. That is when alarm bells rang in my mind and in my parents' minds but sadly, not loud enough. We could see that the cleaning was excessive and beyond reasonable limits, but regrettably, we attributed this to her efforts at being a good mother and foolishly ignored it. She wanted to get the pest treatment done at home, but regrettably, since we were used to living among ants and since this was less than a paltry issue for us, we paid no heed to her request.

These things, I think, were the beginning of minor strife between Sonal on the one side and my family on the other, with me sandwiched in between. I would, naturally, want to keep both sides happy but would not be able to manage either. This is so typical of a married couple living with the boy's parents in India. There are some disagreements; the parents want one thing, the wife wants another and the son/husband almost shudders at the thought of having to arbitrate. I never thought it would happen to me, but soon one of the things I started hoping for when I would leave the office every evening was peace at home, and no situation where I have to be caught in the crossfire.

I was still lucky that there was nothing to worry about most times. Almost all evenings that I returned home were happy and joyous. But once in a while, the law of averages would catch up, and things *would* go wrong. Then Murphy would join in, and whatever else could go wrong would also go wrong.

At times like that, when we would have an unresolved and irresolvable issue brewing, I would ask Sonal, '*Do you want to move out of this house? Should we look for a place for ourselves?*'

She would *always* answer in the negative. She still preferred to stay along with my parents all said and done, maybe because of the sense of security of living with elders. The idea of living alone and managing the house on her own seemed like an onerous task to her, and she preferred the sporadic spats to moving out altogether.

Just about then, in a similar situation – that of being caught in the crossfire between parents and wife, someone known to us committed suicide. On a particularly harsh morning, after a nasty fight between his mother and wife, in which he felt trapped because he could not afford to take sides for fear of antagonizing one or the other party, this man went into the kitchen, picked up a bottle of pesticide and gulped it down. Then he went and told his mother that he had consumed poison. There was apparently a flurry of activity with salt water being given to him so that he could regurgitate the poison out of his system and so that he could be saved but that was not to be. The poison had already entered the blood, and he gave up after a brief struggle and died.

We had gone for the funeral, and it was a piteous sight. The thought that the one who dies, dies but leaves the rest of his loved ones miserable hit us hard. We saw his wife, clad in white (widows wear white in India), crying uncontrollably and his sisters trying to placate her. His eight-year-old daughter could not understand what was going on and played about in innocent ignorance. And his mother! Oh, she was a sight. She was in complete shock for the most part of the day, babbling to herself about how good her son was. When they were finally going to take his body to the cemetery, her bubble burst, and she started wailing. It was terribly heart-rending. I still hear her wails in my mind sometimes.

This incident put the fear of losing a son in my mother's mind, irrational though it was, for I can never see myself contemplating such a cowardly exit, and she brought it up. The only feasible solution (despite my vociferous assertions that I wasn't the least bit suicidal) we could arrive at was to move out of the house. I also didn't want to belabor the point too much because even to me, it seemed like a good idea to be moving out and staying separately, fights or no fights. Finally, that was the consensus. So, we decided to move out.

But I was apprehensive about the impending move as well. The same was also once voiced by my father. My father has always been super perceptive. Not to mention very intelligent. As a kid, I have always idolized him for all that he was. Strong, mature, unshakeable – the veritable Rock of Gibraltar. *My daddy strongest!* I am always amazed by his sagacity, almost as if he is peeping into my mind and echoing what I feel. If this was a comic caper, my jaw would be dropping in incredulity, and I would be saying, '*how the hell do you know?*' This was one such time. So, when he articulated the same concern, I also knew that I wasn't the only one worrying. So, I had to ask Sonal,

'*Sonal, how will you manage the whole house which will be larger, when we move, if one room in this house is taking you so much time to clean?*'

She said evenly, '*Since the new house will be my own, I will not need to spend so much time cleaning it every day. I will buy a house with no ants in it, and since I will also keep it clean from the very beginning, it will not be as bad as it is here.*'

I may not have totally believed what she said, but I knew that she would definitely keep the new house as per her own standards of cleanliness and, therefore, perhaps, just perhaps, it would not need such excessive cleaning regularly. I hoped against hope that it would pan out that way, and I let it go. In retrospect, it was another big mistake to have ignored it.

With her aversion becoming increasingly visible, I had also started doing things to ensure that she didn't have to encounter ants. So, even during my house hunt, I had rejected an apartment that I liked only because there were ants in the apartment. This was a largish apartment in Malad, on the first floor, large rooms with a small terrace. It was close to one of the largest malls in Malad, very conveniently located. Everything seemed nice to me until I saw the ants in the kitchen. Now it could be because the apartment until then was a bachelor pad with a bachelor's stereotypically low standards of neatness. Or it could be that there really were going to be a lot of ants in the apartment. I wasn't going to spend on that apartment to find out which of the two it was. So, it was dropped like a ton of bricks.

Finding an apartment that one likes and that fits in one's budget is, in any case, an arduous task in Mumbai. Then to reject a place, one likes just because there are ants in it? I should have woken up then. But even then, it was a passing thought, and the rejection was also subconscious. There was still no consciousness that my action was an overreaction, governed by what had now moved from a simple aversion to a full-blown fear of ants in Sonal.

The house hunt took its own time too. We saw many apartments, some falling short in some areas, some in others. We saw some very good apartments and some horrible ones too. We saw one apartment that was in the building right next to ours. But that apartment had not been lived in for years and had so much trash in it that Sonal rejected it just to eschew the effort that would go into cleaning the apartment. Back then, I was irritated with her for not seeing the intrinsic value of the flat and for only bothering about the temporary filth there. But now, I understand. She would have been so worried about the ants there that she would just not have been able to say yes to it, even at half the price. After rejecting a good many apartments, we finally found an apartment (a modest 1 BHK) that Sonal and all of us liked. We finally bought our own apartment.

Come 2005, we moved to our new apartment in Andheri, a suburb in Mumbai. My first large purchase. My first house. Oh, how thrilled we were when I finally put a name plate on the door that bore my name. *Sunil Punjabi*. I gleamed. But the move into the apartment had been made with some uncertainty. Moving away from living in a joint family had its pros and cons for Sonal. The biggest con, as already mentioned, was that Sonal was entirely on her own. She would now have to do everything herself. She always doubted herself and suffered from a diminished self-image. She had never managed a house on her own. This apartment would be entirely her responsibility, and she wasn't very sure she would be able to do justice to it.

She would express her doubts frequently, get stressed and state that she wasn't ready to shoulder the whole burden. She would ask me often,

'*What if I'm not able to handle it?*'

'*We shall see. I'm sure you will be able to handle it*', I would say.

I had no doubts that she would be able to. I was also there to help her if there was any required. It was our own nest, and I was happy to build it straw by straw.

The most significant pros were privacy and independence, among other things. Because no matter what, whether justified or not, Sonal just didn't feel free enough to do what she wanted in my parents' house. For whatever she wanted to do, she felt obligated to seek permission. Obviously, there were times when the two women in the house, (my mother and Sonal) didn't agree upon the course of action. Both wanted to do different things, and it was a question of taking sides. *Ek taraf kuaan doosri taraf khaai.* Damned if I did, damned if I didn't.

So, this moving away suited us well. There was no one to tell Sonal what to do and what not to do. She was in all respects the mistress of the house and had a free hand in deciding what went and what didn't. I was happy to finally provide her the freedom she wanted. For a couple of years, but for a few hiccups, things seemed to move along just fine too. We bought whatever Sonal wanted went out as many times as she wanted to. She woke up when it suited her (not that she is a late riser, but there was no obligation to wake up early for the sake of keeping up appearances), and we slept late, watched TV, movies, etc. as much as we wanted to.

It is not as if there are any restrictions one faces when living with parents. But the self-inflicted social pressure of measuring up to anyone living with you is so high that you feel constrained. Sonal felt it more because she had moved from her house to ours. I didn't realize it much that I was feeling it (because I was still in the same house that I had stayed in all my life). Still, after moving into a new apartment of my own, I also began to feel the tautness in my demeanor relaxing. I felt more in control and, consequently, easier. The aversion (as I saw it) to ants continued, but it didn't seem to have assumed scary proportions just then. Or I was plainly ignorant, not even knowing if there was anything that I needed to worry about or keep an eye out for. In fact, there were many 'normal' things that we did in the first couple of years that started becoming impossibilities for Sonal as the affliction began taking deeper roots.

CHAPTER IV

Sonal

"'When I tell you that you're beautiful, I don't just mean your appearance. I mean all of you; who and what you are, is beautiful.' - Steve Maraboli"

Let me take a step back and describe Sonal to lay the foundation of how she was as a person before all this happened. Picture-pretty and well groomed (five feet four inches tall, slim, fair, and with almost oriental features), well painted nails, neither too much make-up on face nor too little, always well dressed. Seldom have I met a person who upon looking at Sonal's picture or upon meeting her, has not remarked about how pretty she is, even sexy). She is that one person whom everybody loves and who loves everybody. Not a bad bone in her body, not one. Soft-spoken. Respectful. Unargumentative. Genial. Exuding endless bonhomie.

Forever willing to help, forever going out of her way to make others feel comfortable. Despite being from a well-to-do family and never having had to lift a finger at home, she managed beautifully and uncomplainingly in our simple, middle-class household. She didn't ever worry about how much money I was making. Her demands were too little, if any. She sometimes questioned the family's decisions but never went against them; she offered her opinion but willingly obeyed the general consensus. She never had it in her to argue and go against any of us because it seemed that she never needed to. She seemed forever happy to agree and be agreeable.

This was a significant relief to me because I didn't ever want to be in a situation where I could not meet my wife's basic expectations from marriage. I believed (and still do) that since after marriage, the girl leaves her house to live with her husband and sometimes (as in our case) with the entire joint family, it becomes imperative for the husband to provide maximum support and every possible comfort to the wife in a house full of near-strangers. Even if it means that he has to sacrifice his own comfort. I learnt it from my father through his actions, and I wanted to be the husband to my wife that my father was to my mother. So, I was happy that she seemed to blend well into the family fabric and I believed I was doing a good job.

You could find Sonal participating in a gathering but not going over the top. She would be involved in the arrangements in every possible way, even if she were not the hostess. In fact, at parties, she would more often be seen helping set it up and run it rather than eating, dancing or behaving like a party-goer. Everyone would insist that she make herself comfortable and sing paeans in her glowing praise for being so helpful. She would humbly smile and continue her efforts.

Her idea of fun was an evening with friends or family. She was the one who always kept urging me to make get-together plans with my cousins or friends. She would also arrange get-togethers with her cousins as and when she could. She loved movies as much as the next person and I'd find myself inside a cinema theatre far more often than I did when I was single. Since I enjoyed watching movies too, we bonded well over these outings, and the more I spent time with her, the more I loved her.

Sonal didn't complain about being one of the seven members (my parents, my brother, *bhabhi* and niece, and the two of us) in the household living in a relatively small 2 BHK apartment. She had come from a family of four living in a two-storey duplex house, after all. I'm not sure I would have been so accommodating in her place. But, none of us was used to living in a cramped environment like that either. For quite a while, my brother lived in Bhopal and moved to Mumbai with his family not too long back. When my brother moved back to Mumbai, the place suddenly became overcrowded. Then with Sonal coming in, it became even more so.

So, everyone was uncomfortable with the human density per square foot in the house and, consequently, the lack of privacy at home. Including Sonal, I'm sure, but she never complained. After a month or so of living in such a congested manner, my brother and his family moved to a rented apartment about half a kilometre away. . That finally accorded us some much-needed breathing space. The apartment finally appeared larger and more spread out, the spaces wider. We were happy to finally walk into the apartment without bumping into each other or stepping on each other's toes and talk without the apprehension of being overheard.

Sonal was a good person at heart and believed that everyone else was too. She didn't have a bad thing to say about anyone and thought that no one would say anything bad about her. We were once at a traffic signal, and an urchin came up to us begging for alms. When I asked her to go away without giving her anything, she pointed her hand in my direction, muttered something unintelligible and went away. Sonal saw this and sweetly said, '*Thank you,*' after the girl had left. I was amused, and I asked her if she knew what the girl had said. She said that she didn't. Amusedly, I told her that she had probably abused us and asked Sonal why she saw to thank her. To which Sonal said simply and pleasantly, '*Since I don't know what she said, why should I assume she said anything bad? Why don't I just assume that she said something good about us?*'

Why not, indeed? Valid point. Another simple life lesson learnt.

Sonal has, however, also always been of the meek variety. Not too worldly-wise. Not comfortable with a lot of things. Soon I realized that she was completely dependent upon me for most things such as bank work, planning vacations, general chores like paying utility bills, getting work done from plumbers, electricians, etc. Sadly, she never showed initiative to update herself by learning these essential new skills. These were small things for me in the beginning. Still, later on, her inability to do these things, her unwillingness to learn them and her leaning on me over them began to peeve me. I used to think that these were so bloody simple, and for a 21st-century urbanite, not knowing these should be considered a crime. Out of irritation at her ineptitude at simple tasks, I often broached the topic with her, and she would just brush it off as something she couldn't be bothered with. That would bug me more.

She was also always uncertain about talking to strangers. Almost immediately after we got married, in early 2003, I had to travel to Chennai and Bangalore for work, and I took Sonal along. I loved Bangalore, and I thought it would be an excellent place for her to visit. Plus, we would get to be together, barring the time I spent at work. We were travelling by train from Mumbai, and as these things go, we soon got to talk to the people sitting in our bogey. A small family of three amiable people – an Indian woman married to a non-Indian man and their three-year old son. Odin, his name was, and he was cute as a button. Odin was the ice breaker for us. His antics had all of us in splits and got Sonal, who is most fond of little children, cooing. She was happy to spend time with him but remarkably (as I noted back then) hesitant to talk to the couple, including the woman. This reticence with also the woman intrigued me. I asked her about it later, and she admitted to feeling diffident.

'*I can't chat with people because I am scared I will make a mistake*', she said nervously.

'*You should at least make an attempt to talk to the woman. She seems kind of nice. What kind of a mistake would you make anyway?*' I queried.

Encouraged by my assurance that I would handle it if anything went wrong, she did make an attempt to talk to the woman. But it amounted to just answering the woman's questions and that too in sub-audible monosyllables. But it was an effort, which I duly acknowledged. After that episode, I repeated, '*Wherever we are, whomever we are with, you talk to them. Do not worry about making mistakes. I will handle the mistakes for you.*'

After that, she did make attempts to be a part of conversations and provide her inputs. Which was good. Although she was far from loquacious, she was at least making an honest and earnest attempt, which would warm me towards her.

Sonal's upbringing has been mired in complexes and fears. She has always been scared of a variety of things such as lizards, cockroaches, dogs, talking to strangers and so on. The fear of lizards in her house is stuff that stand-up comic skits are made of. Everyone, without exception, in her home is thoroughly petrified of lizards. On one occasion, we visited another of Sonal's cousins who stayed in this old apartment building in Bandra. The atmosphere was of general levity and everything was fine until almost the end. When we were leaving and descending the stairs, in the crevices of the severely cobwebbed and cracked-in-many-places ramshackle staircase, a poor lizard lost its balance and the faculties of its adhesive feet that allow it to walk on walls and ceilings and fell down. Worse, it fell right on Sonal's head.

How she had jumped almost out of her skin in fear is something I can never forget. It was hilarious, at least for me, but I dared not laugh. After that, she was tormented for a while, brushing an imaginary lizard off her head repeatedly until her nerves calmed down. That night, I was reading and slept late while Sonal had slept off. Such was the impact of that lizard on her and such was her fear that even in her sleep, she relived the horror, whimpered and tried to brush the imaginary lizard off of her head.

Another incident involving a lizard as the central character took place at my in-laws' house one day. A lizard was lurking on the wall somewhere, and someone happened to see it. *Lizard!* Someone shrieked. The ruckus that ensued was straight out of a slap-stick movie. People running helter-skelter trying to get away from the lizard. One person trotting in this room, the other scampering away into the kitchen, yet another walking away with a modicum of dignity into one corner, scared but not willing to admit. At the risk of sounding immodest, I have never feared any insects or reptiles. So, when this lizard made an appearance, it was the perfect chance for me to be the hero. Among my many failings is one that I never give up an opportunity to impress.

Carpe diem! I seized the day by calmly walking up to the lizard, cupping it in my hand and grabbing it to prevent it from escaping. I ever-so-calmly asked people around, '*What do you want me to do with it?*'

I was enjoying every moment of their discomfiture and my complete control. '*Throw it, throw it*', they exclaimed in horror-imperative.

In Bruce 'cool-dude' Willis' style, I walked up to the kitchen window and threw the lizard out of the window amidst gasps of awe and newly developed respect. I all but took a bow. Boy, did I feel like a hero then!

Back to Sonal, though. What do you think are the chances of having someone like the person I have just described having a defiant streak in her? Strangely, she was a fire brand when it came to defending what was right, according to her. She was very sure of her opinions (when she had them) and didn't care about who thought what when she had to express them. Oscar Wilde once said, '*Most people are other people. Their thoughts are someone else's opinions, their lives a mimicry, their passions a quotation.*' Sonal didn't fall in that definition. If she liked an actor, you could be sure she would like him regardless of how many people think otherwise. Same, if she liked a movie, others didn't. You could be trashing the film in a group in front of her. But if she liked it, she wouldn't keep quiet for fear of being branded a fool. She would declare that it was a good movie.

She mainly was her own person, without any embarrassment about others' opinion of her. This was at once a remarkable and sometimes embarrassing quality because she would sometimes be a misfit in a group. I often wondered whether I should have told her not to express her views in a group if it was not the general view. Even as I write this, it sounds phony to me to make such a suggestion. I reasoned that she may very well be the only person who was being herself without considerations of fear or favor in that gathering. Asking her to be fake because others were either fake or of a different opinion was downright petty. Thankfully, I haven't given in to my own phoniness so far.

Also, if you looked for Sonal in a forum where it came to the protection of women's rights and related subjects, you would likely see her right in the front seats. Vocal. Maybe soft-spoken, but self-assured. Once when we were in Bangalore, we were returning from a movie late at night. She happened to see a few people which I missed, and she said to me with unmistakable concern in her voice,

'I think a few boys are harassing a girl. Turn the car around.'

'What?'

'Turn the car around, now!'

It amazed me to see the deadpan resolve in her eyes, finely blended with concern that would entertain no disagreement. I turned. When we reached the corner, however, those kids were not there. They were probably friends and were engaging in some ribbing. But if it had been anything else, I am pretty sure she would have been the first to step out of the car to accost the culprits. If she ever sees a girl being harassed, she would be the first person to take up cudgels for the girl without regard to personal safety.

At times like this, she would say, *'Main nahin darti in baaton mein kisise'*, (I don't fear anyone in such matters).

Where did she get such spunk from? What was it that made her tick? What was it about her that made her so singularly contradictory? Whereas she was a meek, submissive, almost slavish kind of person in ordinary life, she was a tigress in matters such as these. If only there was an equalizer in her brain, I thought. Something that needed some fine-tuning to ensure that she wasn't as timid as she was in ordinary company. Maybe some internal weighing machine would enable her to move some of her aggression in matters of femininity to day-to-day life, to create a balance.

Sonal had also always been a malleable person but with a spine. She never said no to try new things out. Or if she did, she would agree after a little bit of persuasion. On one of our earliest vacations, she had also agreed to try out paragliding much as she was scared. We were in Pachhmari (a small hill station in Madhya Pradesh). It is a fairly non-commercialized hill station with a few exciting places to see and vast expanses of uncultivated, un-encroached land. We had stepped out for a stroll and chanced upon a camp that was offering a paragliding ride. It was the penultimate day of the camp too. We watched from a distance for a little while. We saw people being fitted with a uniform and getting harnessed, to a parachute. With the help of a fast-moving wagon and the wind, people would rise up in the air because of the parachute. It seemed like a fun thing to do, and being the adrenaline junkie that I am, I wanted to do it too. I have always been fond of adventure sports. I've ticked quite a few sports off my list, including Bungee jumping but hadn't paraglided, and I wasn't about to let go of the chance. Sonal, however, was hesitant. She was rather scared.

I declared that I wouldn't do it either if she didn't do it. She had seen how eager I was to do it. So, even if against her wishes, she reluctantly agreed to do it. I was all excited, like a small child. What an exhilarating ride it was. I got strapped and waited for that one jerk when I would be pulled into the air by the wagon. Sure enough, when the play of the rope that held me was over, I felt a lurch and the wagon suddenly took me up in the air. There I was, rising up in the air, a strong and cool wind caressing my entire body, watching the trees, people and houses below me become tinier and tinier every second. After a few thrilling seconds, the descent began, and I soon touched the ground (or rather, stumbled and fell as my landing was less than perfect – not quite the James Bondish landing I had visualized for myself, but oh well). Another check box was checked from my 'Things to do before I die' list. While walking back to base, I felt like Tom Cruise from Mission Impossible. In uniform with a helmet by my side, heading back to my Katie Holmes. The only thing missing was the pair of Ray-Bans.

Then it was Sonal's turn to get suited up. If she was scared, she didn't show it. She was given a smaller pink overall and a smaller helmet which she wore, and she looked pretty even in the misshapen uniform. She looked at me nervously for comfort. I told her to relax. That she should just enjoy the ride. With a whoop, she was off too. I had been kindly allowed by the organizer to climb into the wagon to reach the other end and be there to receive Sonal when she landed. Sonal's landing was also botched up, and she fell too, but the main thing was that she had done it. She had paraglided, something that she wouldn't have imagined even in her wildest dreams that she would do in her life. I was so proud of her and so enamored with her spirit, flexibility and accommodating nature.

For all her good and bad, we were a happy family. We lived a near-idyllic existence. The four of us my parents, Sonal, and I got along fabulously well. We ate together and did small things together. Sonal and my mother would watch TV together and discuss their soaps at length. We also played Scrabble every evening, all four of us. We would finish dinner, and then the Scrabble board would come out of the closet every evening like clockwork. That would be an hour or two of solid family bonding. She wasn't very good at first, not having ever played it with her parents or friends, but soon she picked the game up very well. Though she was new to the game, she put up a good fight most days. Sometimes, she even won.

For the first six months of our married life, Sonal and I hadn't argued even once. One day at a client's office, the client (whom I had told about my recent marriage) asked me,

'*How is it going? And for how long have you been married now?*'

'*Very well. And I've been married for six months now*', I crowed, exultantly.

'*Wonderful. If the first six months of your marriage go well, your life ahead should be smooth too*', he philosophized.

I hoped then that he was correct and mentally congratulated myself for having crossed that milestone.

CHAPTER V

Celebrating Festivals

"'Live every day as if it is a festival. Turn your life into a celebration.'
- Anonymous"

The advantage of staying in our own house was the independence that came with it. Like for the first three years, we celebrated *Ganesh Chaturthi* at home. *Ganesh Chaturthi* is an Indian festival where the idol of *Ganesha*, the Elephant God, is worshipped for 11 days. *Ganesh Chaturthi* starts with the installation of statues of Lord *Ganesha* in temporary temple-like structures and ends with the immersion of the same statue in water. Some individuals also buy their own small clay statue for their homes. . After 1.5, 5, 7 or 10 days immerse it either in a tub at home or in some external body of water, amid joyous celebrations. During these eleven days, *modak*, the favorite sweet of Lord *Ganesha* and other sweets are consumed in large quantities and adorning the *Ganesha* idol with flowers is the norm. Also, people visit each other's houses to pay obeisance and bring more sweets, fruits and flowers.

Sonal had always wanted to keep a *Ganesha* during Ganesh Chaturthi at home. Still, she couldn't do so at her parents' house because her father was not in favor. Nor could she keep it at my parents' house as she hadn't ever felt comfortable even to broach the subject. But she had told me that she would do so when we moved to our own apartment. Even if for just a day and a half. I thought it would be nice to have a pious atmosphere at home and have so many visitors. Shlok would be happy to meet his extended family and eat the sweets that would be part of the *prasad*. I was also willing to observe the rules that went with the festival. The light in the room where the idol is kept could not be switched off, even at night, and the idol could never be left alone in the room. Someone had to always be present. This is out of respect for the deity. Since one has invited Him home as a guest, He needs to be treated like one. Despite not enjoying sleeping in a room with the light switched on, I was willing to do it since it made Sonal happy.

For three years (2007 to 2009), we brought *Ganesha* home. For one and a half days each year. All the *poojas* that were to be done were done as per norms with no stone unturned. Since Sonal belongs to a gregarious family, as expected, many extended family members came over to offer their obeisance. Many of my friends and colleagues from the office. Shlok was in playschool then. As part of his playschool routine, little children in his class were taken for a field trip to visit some Ganesh *pandal*. Since our apartment was closest to the play school, the entire rabble of children, teachers and helper-maids had come over.

We had close to 150 people coming over in two days. As expected, there was too much food cooked, eaten (and spilled), too many sweets brought, distributed and eaten (and spilled), too many flowers offered to the idol (and spilled), too many fruits distributed and offered as *prasad* (and spilled). All of this seemed pretty normal to me. After all, with so many people at home, how could you expect to have a clinically clean environment anyway? It was an unavoidable part of celebrating such a massive festival at home and a minor irritant that is all.

In the first year, it was normal for Sonal too. She did everything that she needed to, too. With great flair. No skipping rituals. No disrespect to God or any visitor in any manner. No skimping on the *prasad*. While it is normal to offer maybe a fruit or a sweet as *prasad* to every visitor, Sonal would have none of that. She didn't want anyone to go hungry. She hired a temporary chef for two days to cook proper meals and ensured that whoever came to visit ate well and went. If they couldn't wait, they would be given a take-away bag. Sonal handled all the guests with a flourish.

In the second year (2008), while there wasn't the largest scale of the first year, there wasn't any cutting of corners either. She didn't keep a cook, but the *prasad* was ordered from a snacks vendor, and each visitor was loaded with it when he left the house. The poojas the *aarti*s were also done to perfection. She gave away more than she got. None of this was done to show off her largesse, though it sounds like that when I am writing this. Sonal doesn't have a single ostentatious bone in her body. This is just her way of doing everything right. Of not leaving anything halfway. Of doing more, rather than less. Of erring on the right side of caution. Of near-perfection.

Shlok's birthdays would be very meticulously planned too. The guest list would be appropriately chalked out. Information would go out well in advance. The venues, the menu, the decorations and the cake would all be arranged for in time. The return gifts that would be given to the children who attended the birthday party would be bought depending upon the age and gender of the child. Nothing was one-size-fits-all for Sonal. It was remarkable. It was noticed by a lot of people and commented upon too. Her perfection in planning and administration. But I am going off track. The crux is that there would be cake and sweets and food, which she would not just tolerate but partake of too.

Even during the other festivals like *Diwali* (the festival of lights), *Holi* (the festival of colors) and *Raksha Bandhan* (the day when sisters tie a *rakhi*, which is a wrist band to their brothers for their protection), there would be enough sweets that would be brought home. Chocolates during Christmas. Every year, we also keep a Christmas tree to build some fantasy in Shlok's life. All these occasions brought Sonal in contact with sweets. For the first two years, she managed this tryst with sweets and festivals and celebrations beautifully.

Two years only. Third-year onwards (in 2009), every festival or celebration was a maelstrom for Sonal because by then, unbeknownst to any of us, the aversion to ants, which we hadn't yet classified into a full-blown disorder, had firmly taken roots in Sonal's consciousness and meant to stay. She suffered a lot in the last year of Ganesh Chaturthi. The effort to see the event through and not let me know how stressed she was, exhausted her. I wasn't aware of it, and Sonal kept it from me. Perhaps having realized that her actions under the influence of her mental state were both incorrect and excessive, Sonal had steadfastly chosen to be disingenuous about her condition with me. On the surface, life seemed to be pretty normal.

It was only later that she told me that she had half a mind not to celebrate *Ganesh Chaturthi* in year three at all. But she believed that once you begin, you should celebrate it for a minimum of three years, and hence she didn't want to break the tradition and incur God's wrath. Such orthodoxy! So, she foolishly gave in to the superstition and willed herself to keep the *Ganesha* for the third year as well.

Had I known that she was suffering so much and that not going through the silly ritual of completing three years would help her, I wouldn't have allowed her to, tradition or no tradition. I am not a person given to superstitions at all and my belief in the existence of God apart (of which I am an unabashed heretic, not subscribing to many dogmas in the name of religion, such as women not being allowed inside temples during menstruation and other such annoying rituals), I believe that no God can be a cruel God. He would not dole out punishment at the drop of a hat. He would be omniscient and considerate enough to know His devotees' problems. He would surely not punish them just because they could not stick to some silly three-year custom, which was anyway man-made. But now I feel I was daft not to have seen it. The signs were all there. I was just blind to them. I guess something more extensive and more in-the-face was required to make me sit up and take note.

This event with the two ants at Diwali was as much in-the-face as it could get. After this frightful experience, we realized that Sonal needed professional help, and she needed it fast. The first and the only thing I could think of then was to source out the number of the only reputed psychiatrist - I will call her AA- I knew of back then and fix up an appointment for Sonal with her. I discussed it with Sonal, and she agreed to meet her - which was a good thing. At least she was not running away from it anymore. I was relieved when she said yes to see a psychiatrist.

It was one of the best decisions of her life. I am, in a way, very thankful to her for not having resisted it then. We sourced out the number and fixed up an appointment. I was determined to see this through with Sonal. I didn't want her to feel alone and uncared for at a time when she needed the support of her loved ones the most. Hence, I got Sonal to fix up an appointment only when it would be possible for me to go with Sonal to the shrink. I wasn't going to let her go alone. One, for solidarity (that we were in this together), and two, I knew she wouldn't be able to handle it alone. She would not ask the right questions or enough questions if she felt intimidated. Nor would she be able to put forward her case very well, and there was a strong chance of that if she went alone. So, I was going to go with her.

On the day of the appointment, which was my birthday, we headed out. For our first-ever visit to a psychiatrist. Certainly not how I had envisaged spending my birthday. It was a strangely unnerving, butterflies-in-the-stomach kind of feeling, which came out of uncertainty about what was in store for us. What had we gotten ourselves into and where would it end? With a silent prayer that hopefully, this was a minor hiccup and would get taken care of by supposedly one of the best psychiatrists in Mumbai. With a hope that we could get on with our lives in no time.

Little did we know that we had a personal typhoon in store for us that would not only send our lives spiralling out of control but also challenge the strength of our relationships, our will and our survival skills! Sonal's OCD was soon going to assume complete control, force us into an alternate way of life by causing relentless repetition of her rituals - Ctrl Alt Repeat - to a near-breaking point.

CHAPTER VI

The Experience With AA

"'You control your destiny — you don't need magic to do it. And there are no magical shortcuts to solving your problems.' – Merida in Brave"

Given that AA is supposedly among the best in the city, with so many articles in the newspapers carrying quotes from her and her opinion being sought on most issues related to mental health, the experience with her was disappointing. But at that point in our lives, when things seemed to be falling apart from all sides, I wasn't very discerning to make a judgment call about whether to continue with AA or not. We strove to free Sonal of her predicament, and AA seemed to be the default option. I have also believed and propagated that faith in one's doctor is an absolute must. One cannot operate without having faith in one's doctor. They, after all, know more than you do, which is why you are visiting them, to begin with. What is the point of going to the doctor and not believing that their treatment will be effective?

The first experience at the shrinks was quite unlike how I had expected it to be, given that until then, all the exposure I had had to the chambers of a psychiatrist was only from movies. First of all, we were made to wait in the waiting room endlessly. Who shows that in the movies? We sat there with as much patience as we could muster under the situation, wondering when we would be called in. We, on our part, had reached on time. So, it was poor time management on their part because I saw way too many patients patiently waiting for their turns too. The first impression was not very good. I was desperate to meet AA to understand the problem with Sonal and get an assurance from her that it was curable and would be cured in a short time. I had expected to be led into her chambers after just a short wait (if not straightaway) and attack the problem at the core. Isn't that always our expectation? That everything will go right? That our conversations will go exactly as planned? That our problems will have simple solutions and will be easily remedied? When we think of how some situations will play out, we always expect things to go without a hitch. These expectations are almost always unmet and this time was no different. We had to wait. Far longer than we would have liked to.

I think after an hour or so of waiting, which seemed far more than that, with Sonal fretting and Shlok getting bored, we were approached by a brisk woman who handed us a few forms. Sonal was asked to fill them in. Really? Couldn't that at least have been done sooner? They aimed to get to know her a little, her medical history, her opinion on certain things, her reaction in certain situations - assessing her general mental health. Sonal, who balks at writing any 'test', found this route objectionable and didn't want to fill the forms. I had to spend the next five minutes convincing her that it was required. I finally managed to cajole (read badger) her into filling the forms.

She took her time filling in the forms, muttering under her breath all the while. Someone came and relieved us of those forms. We waited some more. A lot more, in fact. I guessed that the forms were being checked inside, and a summarized assessment was being made by AA's team for her quick look through. To give her a general idea of what she was dealing with. After another eternity, by which time, both Sonal and I were on edge, not Shlok though, who despite being bored was a perfect angel and did not trouble us at all, we were summoned inside AA's room. We saw an affable-looking, short-haired, middle-aged woman sitting in a fairly cluttered room with an even more cluttered desk. There were all sorts of knick-knacks on the table with just about enough space for her blotter. There was a recliner in her room, like you see in the movies.

Here it comes, I thought to myself. She would ask me to step out and get Sonal to narrate her tale of woe. But she didn't ask me to wait outside. Huh? What about doctor-patient confidentiality? What about privacy for Sonal if she wanted to vent out against me? What about the doctor's need to bond with the patient one-on-one? Wouldn't she be better served if she had a chance to speak to the doctor alone? I even asked AA if I should wait outside. She smiled and said no. If you say so, I thought to myself wryly. I reasoned, however, that perhaps, she may have wanted Sonal to feel comfortable, and if it meant that Sonal needed to have me around, so be it.

I thought she would make Sonal lie down on the recliner and let her talk, which didn't happen either. Double huh? Somehow, in my mind's eye I always thought that a patient at a psychiatrist's clinic would be most comfortable and would relax only if allowed to lie down on the recliner and vent out with eyes shut while the psychiatrist took notes. The room would be large, clean and minimalistic, with dim lights, an impressive-looking bookshelf behind and soft, relaxing pipe music soothing frayed nerves. There was no such thing there. Just a functional and cluttered office. Another illusion shattered.

It was a good thing that I was not asked to wait outside because when Sonal was asked to speak about her problem, she wasn't even sure what she should say, probably out of nervousness over what ailed her. So, I helped where I could. Between us, we narrated our entire experience completely asynchronously, in a matter of fifteen minutes. All the tears and suffering, all the struggles, all the fears condensed into fifteen minutes like a soft drink concentrate. To her credit, AA didn't interrupt us when we talked, looked interested and made the customary understanding noises. As soon as we were done, she reached a verdict and pronounced it. '*It is OCD*,' she smiled and said simply.

I was shocked. OCD? '*Are you sure?*' I thought to myself. Because Sonal was only scared of ants. How could it be? I had a vague notion of OCD then, which was restricted to very little information beyond the acronym's expansion. I was momentarily fazed by the declaration. It had seemed like a phobia to me. I was pretty sure she would say Sonal was suffering from Myrmecophobia (fear of ants) or Entomophobia (fear of insects; I had Googled the terms) or some such thing. But she said in a voice that would entertain no arguments or harbor no doubt whatsoever that it was OCD. The conversation had once again not gone my way, and although we didn't understand the impact then, OCD, for some reason, seemed like a bigger problem than the phobias.

When we were in school and college and were not satisfied with our examination results of any of the subjects, we had the option of getting a revaluation done. More often than not, the marks would come out better in the revaluation than they did the first time. For some reason, whenever I'm faced with an outcome to a situation that is unpalatable to me, my first thoughts go to the process of revaluation, and I wonder if there is one possible. Too bad, here it was neither possible nor was there any hope that the results would be any different if, by some miracle, that chance were to be made available to us. Unlike so many words in the English dictionary with multiple meanings, this didn't. This was what it was — Obsessive Compulsive Disorder.

In the next couple of minutes, though, we were whisked out of the room, armed with a prescription of anti-OCD drugs and 1500 rupees lighter. AA didn't spend any time explaining the how's and why's. Well, not much, in any case. She didn't ask Sonal if she would be comfortable taking medication or would she rather undergo counseling. If there was a choice, that is. She didn't even make us aware of the options we had. When we had decided to go to a psychiatrist for Sonal's treatment, she and I had discussed it. The general decision was to avoid medicines if we could and just try to eliminate the problem through counseling and therapy.

AA didn't ask. She also didn't tell us what needed to be done and what needed to be avoided. After so many years of living with Sonal and after experiencing the disorder second-hand, I now know that there are enough do's and don'ts in OCD for a sufferer to follow. Worst of all, she had no specific answers to my basic questions – what was I expected to do to help Sonal? How was I supposed to behave? Was I supposed to allow her excesses, or was I supposed to stop her from giving in to them? Which ones was I supposed to allow? Which ones was I supposed to stop her from doing? She said something inane like – continue to support her. Since OCD is a behavioral disorder and correct care could very well be the difference between the sufferer getting better or getting worse, the least she could have done is to make me aware of the whole gamut of possibilities. She didn't. My questions went unanswered, and we were at the mercy of the medicines for Sonal to get better. To feel better.

Right after the diagnosis and the prescription, AA was all but dismissive, as if she wanted us out of the room fast. As if, Sonal's situation was contagious, and if she were in the same room as Sonal, she would contract it too. Maybe she had other patients to attend to. Which she did, going by the crowd in the waiting room. Or perhaps, she belatedly realized that she had overrun her schedule and wanted to catch up on the lost time. Or, I also cynically thought, maybe she just wanted to make more money by meeting as many patients as she could and entertaining us any further by answering our naive, amateurish questions would keep her from doing that.

So, we left. Feeling confused. Didn't know whether to be satisfied with the visit or not. I looked at Sonal to see if she was happy with the interaction. It was evident in her countenance that Sonal, too, wasn't satisfied. She didn't think that the doctor listened to her enough. She didn't think she got to talk enough. Get it off her chest. She felt that the effort to bond that the doctor should make with the patient was missing. She thought too that the doctor didn't answer her questions to assuage her fears and befuddlement. Where was the attempt to make the sufferer feel comfortable? Where was the effort to counsel the sufferer and give her the courage that she had lost on account of her fears? Where was the opportunity provided to the sufferer to relieve her burden, at least in part, by speaking out her fears and experiences? Where was the empathy? Where was the compassion?

One simple footnote in the fine print of 'How to deal with OCD sufferers – a guide for dummies' should be that the sufferer does not want to be talked down to. Instructed to do as she is told. Ordered around. Pushed about. She wants to do the talking. She wants someone to reach out to her. Hold her hand. Walk with her. Answer all her questions. Help her with her uncertainties and blow away the clouds of confusion. This was missing with AA. Sonal had all too clearly experienced the void.

I wasn't feeling right about the whole episode. But I just attributed it to our lack of knowledge of the procedure. I realized that a psychiatrist will anyway only prescribe medicines. If we wanted to talk, we should have sought a psychologist. Nevertheless, faith was an essential requirement for the treatment to be effective, and upon my concurrence, Sonal obediently and meekly started following the prescription.

For a few weeks, Sonal did as she was told. That is, take her medicines on time and as per prescription. We went to AA for a couple of sessions more. But every session was a repeat of the first one. Until it began to tell on Sonal. The effort of pretending that things were getting better. Clearly, the experience with AA was not working for us. It did not work for us on two counts, not one. One, Sonal was new to the medication, and her frail body hadn't adjusted itself to the innumerable side effects of the psychiatric drugs. They would cause drowsiness and have her sleep more than she could allow herself to. That is what psychiatric medicines are notorious for, anyway. They have a lot of side effects – loss of appetite, loss of libido, drowsiness, upset stomach, danger to the foetus in case of pregnancy and many others. This was no different then.

Because of the sedative effects of the medicine, Sonal's daily routine was getting affected, which was unacceptable to her because her compulsions (read cleaning routine) had worsened by this time. She would spend nearly three hours every day cleaning the house. In multiple sessions at that, so it would seem longer. She had started buying almost twice as many cleaning agents and cleaning cloths as we did earlier. She would use any cleaning cloth only for a week or ten days before it was discarded. Then every surface of the house would be wiped with a wet cloth, including windows, the window grille, wardrobes, the wall unit, doors, the refrigerator, the washing machine, the microwave oven, the centre table, the chairs, the dining table, the...well, everything. So, it would take a long time for her to finish everything.

Soon, routine tasks like taking care of Shlok, cooking, grocery shopping, etc became burdensome for Sonal and, consequently, secondary. Keeping the house clean (and therefore ant-free) was a top priority (if not the only priority). Everything else that did not contribute to that objective could either wait or be skipped. She went through a harrowing day every day. The worst part was that she couldn't put up her feet and rest, considering all of it a good job done because the following day, the entire routine needed to be followed through, all over again. It was stressful even for me to watch her go through it every day, but there seemed to be precious little that I could do.

I tried to help as much as I could, despite the constraints on my time, due to work. I would get Shlok ready for school and drop him at the school bus stop. So, Sonal would not need to be disturbed to get Shlok to school. When I returned home from work in the evening, I would take charge of Shlok's studies, free-time, games, and entertainment. On weekends and holidays, I would generally ensure that we stay out of Sonal's hair so that she could finish her chores on time and have some time to herself. But the medicines from AA's arsenal didn't help her cause because of the sedative effects. She began to feel more stressed despite the medication and also because of it. No amount of help or talking made a difference, and we were starting to wonder if things were getting better at all. In fact, they seemed to be getting worse.

This had started building resentment in me since I did not understand what was happening and was suddenly feeling overburdened with both office work and house work. Sonal would not make it better because in her state rather than seeking help and trying to make me understand, she would get agitated if I protested and we would end up fighting. We argued a lot and sometimes at the top of our lungs. All in front of a scared, confused and distraught 5 year old. Neither of us could understand how our idyllic existence had gone from utopian to dystopian in such a short span of time. Needless to say, our relationship began to become the sacrificial lamb at OCD's altar.

The other reason AA's treatment didn't work for Sonal as mentioned, was that there was no one-on-one counseling, which Sonal was seeking, more than the medication. Sonal wanted to talk. She wanted someone to listen to her gigantic, insurmountable problem. She needed a professional shoulder to cry on. When the need for counseling was pointed out to AA and a request was made to substitute medicines for just counseling, she told us unequivocally that she couldn't take Sonal off the medication. There was no choice, she said. In fact, she had ostensibly started with a low dosage, and the dosage was going to have to be increased soon. Surprisingly, the suggestion of counseling seemed to be a thought that hadn't struck her.

But to her credit, she did agree to assign a counselor from her clinic to talk to Sonal. I was a little relieved that there would finally be an outlet for Sonal's rants. Sure enough, the next time we went to AA's clinic, instead of meeting her, Sonal met a counselor. A twenty-something, haughty girl who didn't seem rude but not friendly either. Maybe she had taken the doctrine of not getting too attached to her patients a tad too seriously because there was a thin veneer of ice to her. A 'touch-me-not' or rather a 'be-friendly-to-me-not' kind of quality. She was sadly, less than optimal. She met Sonal in a strip of a room that looked more like a staff restroom than anything else. Two more women sat there, chatted away and ate their lunches nonchalantly, oblivious to our presence, discomfort and our obvious need for privacy. Not the right environment for Sonal to feel comfortable to offload her worries.

She gave Sonal certain difficult exercises to do as homework. Sonal found these extremely tough to do and could not do them because they caused her stress. Understandably so, because Sonal was new to the whole treatment and therapy routine and all at once tasks that she had been avoiding for quite some time were given to her to be done as homework, without any hand-holding. She wasn't guided on how to approach the tasks and what to do if she couldn't. She was asked to start buying *mithais*, which we had stopped after that fateful Diwali night. Naturally, she found them difficult to do. She wasn't doing any of that despite having a son who would need those items. Because she could not bring herself to. She obviously wasn't going to be able to start doing that just because the counselor asked her to.

In retrospect, the counselor didn't follow a structured way of doling out the homework at that time. Maybe she was an intern herself. Or a new appointee who didn't have too much experience. I now know that it was all very random and was doomed to failure, even though the approach was correct. The exercises were not graded −from the lowest anxiety-inducing exercises to the highest, the lowest being tackled first. It appeared to me that since the activities were simple for the counselor to perform, she thought that they had to be simple for Sonal as well. Far from understanding the problem Sonal faced in trying to do the exercises and trying to find a better way to deal with it, the counselor would pooh-pooh her fears and be just a shade short of contemptuous of Sonal's failed efforts. She actually got irritated when Sonal told her that she couldn't complete her tasks. The sessions started stressing Sonal out more than they relieved her. The counselor was also not working out. I could see that Sonal was more stressed than ever. She would break down sometimes. She would constantly keep saying that she wouldn't be able to do it. I was powerless to make my wife feel better, and it started worrying me.

With my limited knowledge of the various psychological therapies, I also suggested group therapy to AA. She was, at best, evasive. Maybe she didn't have enough OCD patients to conduct group therapy. Or perhaps she didn't think it was a good option. I thought group-therapy at that time for Sonal would have worked wonders. Then, it was a passing thought. Now, I stand by it. I am pretty sure Sonal would have benefitted through group therapy.

If Sonal is a representative of how OCD sufferers are, having lived with her and having seen her go through the suffering, I know that OCD sufferers relate to the sufferings of others better and draw strength from their efforts. They laud the successes that other sufferers see and sympathize with their failures. They are more likely to listen to people who have gone through similar suffering and emerged victorious than to the pedantic rants of a doctor or a counselor. They seek succor in numbers. What they want most is someone they feel is by their side (a friend) and not someone above them (an authoritative figure). They tend to identify with laymen better than they do with geeks on the subject.

Sonal feels compassionate towards people who suffer from any mental condition. She feels like reaching out and sharing in their sorrow or pain. Group-therapy would have given her strength from the experience of others and confidence to share her own troubles. She would have seen that she wasn't the only one suffering, and perhaps others were suffering more. Or for longer. She would have found an outlet. She could have been both a counselor and a patient in group therapy. But AA was having none of it.

The third reason why AA was not working out was the interminable wait in her office. Only to be seen for ten to fifteen minutes. Often, Sonal had waited in the waiting room for over two hours before she was finally able to see the doctor. Had the medicines and counseling been working, the wait would have been a minor irritant. But since the medicines and counseling were not working, and Sonal felt that she had to get back to do the household chores, waiting at the doctor's office for two hours at a time was unacceptable to her. She would sometimes miss her sessions because the thought of spending so much time waiting seemed like a waste of time, which she felt she would rather spend doing her rituals. When I would get to know of it, I would feel terribly let down and the disappointment would manifest in anger. We would end up arguing again and a power-struggle would become visible. Our exchanges would be of the '*I-will-not-go*' and '*you-will-have-to*' variety. Our conversations had become more argumentative than cooperative.

The interaction with AA and her team and her consequent feeling of inadequacy in holding up wasn't good for her morale, and I was not equipped to handle it. The delay at the doctor's office would serve to increase her anxiety, rather than abate it. So, after a lengthy discussion about the pros and cons, we finally concluded that we needed to see another specialist. Hence, we decided to drop the services of AA and her entourage of counselors altogether.

CHAPTER VII

The Intensity Of The Problem – Glimpse I

"'Strength does not come from winning. Your struggles develop your strengths. When you go through hardships and decide not to surrender, that is strength.' - Arnold Schwarzenegger"

Having gotten to know the name of what ailed Sonal, I started researching on OCD. I did whatever I could do to gain as much knowledge as possible to make life a little more comfortable for Sonal, and in turn, for Shlok and me. Nothing was small enough, nothing insignificant. I tried every trick I could lay my hands upon for some respite.

Some books that I read were written by sufferers who have gained some degree of control over their lives. More power to them. If Sonal were the reading and researching kind, maybe we would have had more books to read, more techniques to discuss and more attempts to be made. There used to be a time when she used to carry a Danielle Steele book under her arm when she met me during our courtship days. She would sometimes read a Chetan Bhagat book. But by now, Sonal had also lost all interest in reading, and there was no sense in expecting her to read and research. I read all I could and picked up whatever I could, but I never came across any books by someone who has lived with the sufferer. Nothing was written from a caregiver's point of view.

I looked up various videos on YouTube.com to share with Sonal to provide a visual frame of reference rather than just textual or verbal. These videos, which cover the obsessions and compulsions of OCD sufferers, gave us a general idea of the sufferer's helplessness. Some of them were scary, some inspiring. I also realized that suffering of one person with OCD is entirely different from the suffering of another.

I watched a video where a teenager spends a couple of hours just grooming his hair in front of the mirror. No matter how well his hair was combed, it was just not good enough for him. I watched another video where someone had to open and shut the door, switch the light on off, wash hands and even make the bed, iron the bed to remove the wrinkles many times until it felt right. Having seen Sonal go through a similar ordeal, it rent the heart to see people suffering like that. Even as I write this, there is an overwhelming urge to reach out to each sufferer with a hug.

But whenever I showed Sonal any of those videos I found, her constant refrain was that since her suffering was different from theirs (and to her, her suffering has always been more severe than anyone else's), it may have been easier for the person in the video to beat the disorder, but it wasn't so for her. Other sufferers may feel the same way. They may feel that the YouTube videos are over-simplifications of a very complex problem. Either the progress shown is exaggerated or the sufferer's situation in the video is not severe to begin with. Isn't it obvious that the videos would have been shot over a long period, and the time between those neat and tidy frames would not have been so easy?

Similar to the 'before and after' ads. I remember seeing a Bullworker exercise equipment ad as a kid. You see a skinny person in the 'before' picture and a muscular one in the 'after' picture. For the before picture to become the after photo, the mere purchase of Bullworker would not be enough. One would need to use it over an extended period to see results. The YouTube videos represented the results with a glimpse of the efforts, not really all the measures required. That made it seem that the sufferers in the video had it easy.

To add to it, in those YouTube videos, there was almost always a doctor or counselor present with the sufferer to help them focus on their therapy. To help them not make any mistakes. To help them stay on track. To course-correct where required. There was one video in particular in which the sufferer was scared of closed spaces initially but after therapy, she was able to travel in an elevator by herself. I found that very inspiring. That video had the constant presence of a doctor. Hence, Sonal set her mind upon the continuous presence of the doctor as an important reason why sufferers overcame their suffering.

She just wasn't able to accept that the doctors in the videos were present only for the shoot and that the sufferers didn't really have a doctor available to them round-the-clock. That they can't have a doctor present at all times. To have a doctor present 24X7 while the sufferer is undergoing therapy is as impossible as it is absurd. But Sonal would not buy the argument and could not relate to any of the sufferers from the videos to draw strength and inspiration from them and firm up her resolve to conquer her own OCD. So, unluckily, we drew a blank there as well. I just couldn't believe Sonal could have become so stubborn. Stubborn to the core. Rigid. Inflexible.

Unyielding. Also sadly, blind to the fact that it was to her detriment.

Sonal's OCD in the meantime was having a free run, and the monster made merry in the jamboree, playing on Sonal's mind and revelling in her pain. Her condition was going from bad to worse. In the book '*Gaza in Crisis*' by Noam Chomsky and Ilan Pappe, Frank Barat uses an Arabic word in the introduction – *Nakbah*, which means catastrophe. So, this is what my beautiful sounding but life-sapping *Nakbah* was. Sonal had developed an aversion to getting anything sweet inside the house by now. Jams, honey and *mithai*s were a strict no-no. As were cakes and cream biscuits.

These items could not even be mentioned at home anymore; forget getting them. Whereas earlier she would make sweets for breakfast (*lola* which is like a sweet *chapatti*, *borat* which is ground *chapatti* mixed with sugar and roasted, and *satpuri* which is a *jaggery* filled *chapatti* – all Sindhi sweet dishes that Shlok had a predilection for), after the OCD, she stopped making these altogether. She replaced them with the relatively unappetizing (for Shlok) *pohe* (puffed rice) and *upma* (a salted breakfast dish made of semolina), much to his disappointment.

Even sugar, the staple sweetener in everyone's houses, was dealt with, with extreme caution in ours. That we had sugar at home was a big achievement in itself. In later years, we had even stopped keeping sugar at home. But I shall cover that later. Sonal was so scared of handling the sugar that the sugar container was almost treated like a ticking time bomb. Gingerly, carefully. The shelf on which the container was to be kept was repeatedly wiped first. The entire container was repeatedly wiped. Repetition is a common characteristic of OCD compulsions. The sufferer does not feel that the work has been done well enough and needs to do it repeatedly. Any interruption in the process gets the sufferer to start believing that the task has not been done at all and she starts doing it again.

Such was the case with Sonal's repetitive wiping too. This was to ensure that there were no microscopic foreign particles stuck either to the bottom of the container or on the shelf. Any small particle that she found needed to be removed lest it makes the container rest less than stably and causes it to topple, thereby spilling the sugar and attracting ants. The small container (which could be literally picked up with two fingers) was picked up using both hands and very gradually to not upset the sugar level in the container; it was lifted to the height of the shelf and placed on the shelf. If she felt that the container was not properly placed for whatever reason, and that would happen many times every day; she would pick it up and keep it down again.

Once again, the entire process of wiping the shelf and the container would start. To keep the container of sugar from the kitchen platform to the shelf would sometimes take Sonal a full 20 minutes, what with the process needing to be repeated *ad nauseam*. The container would anyway hold half the quantity of sugar it could or lesser. So, even if one shook the container, the chances that the sugar would spill out of the container were less than zero. But it was well-nigh impossible to explain that to Sonal.

Up to the point that I hadn't seen this ritual of hers, I didn't know how important it was for her to not shake the container, and how terrifying it was for her if it was. I got to know of it the hard way when we were arguing about something trivial and things escalated to a massive argument one evening. Huge arguments over nothingness were becoming fairly common between us then. I was miffed at Sonal for taking forever to serve dinner. As usual, Sonal was being defiant and unapologetic (even rude) about her ever-increasing rituals. During the particularly heated altercation that followed, I went to the kitchen while her sugar-ritual was in process.

I picked up the sugar container and shook it out of a misplaced sense of idiotic one-upmanship, telling her that I would spill all the sugar at home if she did not stop misbehaving. What happened next was a phantasmagoria of pure horror - stuff that nightmares are made of. I shudder to even think of it. She was yelling at the top of her lungs and crying herself hoarse. She started cursing me for not understanding her plight. I was horrified at the explosive reaction and alarmed at what I had done. I was worried that if she continued, she would rupture an aneurysm. I don't remember if I said sorry, though, to dissipate the situation. I was a stuck-up jerk then, and it is more likely than not that I would have just raised my hands in surrender and walked out of the kitchen, leaving her to do her rituals again without making any efforts to make her feel better. Or express my regret.

But then, after I saw the ritual once, I knew why she had reacted so strongly. Even though giving in to her rituals was not the correct thing to do, the flip side was far too dangerous, and I surely didn't want her to suffer so much as to collapse out of sheer stress. I vowed never to do it again.

In Sonal, I noted a peculiarity that bears mentioning. While sugar, jam and sweets were anathema and hence completely out of bounds, strangely, her fear of sweet things was and continues to be selective. It makes her story even more bizarre and seemingly implausible. While she is scared of sugar and sugar syrups, sweetened soft drinks are fine. She would treat herself to a Fanta from time to time. One of her favorite drinks continues to be *masala* ThumsUp (a cola drink). That is ThumsUp mixed with *Jal jeera masala*. How she is able to drink that is a mystery considering that it is sugar-loaded. She may be scared of cream biscuits and chocolate biscuits (even with miniature chocolate chips), but regular biscuits, even if sweet, present no problem. When we stopped keeping sugar at home altogether, she would use Parle–G Glucose biscuits to sweeten her tea. She would not tolerate even looking at a mango, much less touch it or eat it, but a watermelon would be relished. Some other fruits would be too.

It is good that she can eat these things, but this kind of behavior (selective abhorrence) is nothing short of bizarre. It kind of throws one off track. Putting all sweets in the same category does not work here. People would not be able to understand this partiality to some sweets and would think she was faking it. If she were to be seen sipping a Pepsi one moment and cower at the sight of jam the next moment, no one would accept that she is unwell. No one would believe her or empathize with her. If I weren't living with her and hadn't seen the pain that she has gone through, I would be inclined to disbelieve it too and, as a sum total, be more apathetic. I had even asked her about this. If we could identify why she could tolerate these sweets, we could alter her thinking to include other sweets and help her get rid of her fear. Alas, her responses to questions trying to arrive at the root cause of the discrimination yielded an often ignorant and sometimes haughty '*I don't know*'. As a result, we were nowhere close to a solution while her condition continued to deteriorate.

When she would be stressed, she would also start mumbling under her breath. Her mumbling would begin in a near-whisper and gradually increase in volume until it reached a fevered pitch, and she would start her strident yelling. It was horrific to have a hysterical woman to deal with. It was mentally back-breaking. I also kept wondering what effect it might have on Shlok and how I would insulate him from the possible damage to his yet undeveloped and highly impressionable psyche. Sonal could never distinguish between the right time and the wrong time, and if she felt stressed, which was more or less always those days, she would rant audibly. It could be at home or outside, even in a restaurant or other public places.

I always wondered what our neighbors or the waiters in the restaurants must be thinking about the diatribe they must be hearing. Their opinion wasn't important though. Because although I am not exactly Bohemian (I reside with everyone else in the collective after all), societal acceptance has never ranked very high with me if it interferes with my freedom. But sometimes, it was embarrassing when people stared. Worse, when a casual glance around me showed people who were pretending that they hadn't noticed.

Sonal would be completely oblivious of the potential sniggers her rants might have been evoking. I would sound her off, sometimes loudly and sometimes in hushed whispers through clenched teeth that she was tottering on the brink of insanity and that she should behave herself. I told her about what the neighbors might be thinking. She didn't care. She would defend herself, stating that mumbling was her way of venting her feelings out, making her feel better. It gave her peace. She would yell at me instead for worrying more about the neighbors than about relieving her stress. These would also frequently start off as her mumbling and end in full blown arguments. That wasn't helping. I would try to make peace but it was difficult to manage it amicably. So, after a point, at least for some time, I stopped objecting. Whatever floats your boat, I would think, and drop the matter. *Pax Vobiscum!*

CHAPTER VIII

Homeopathy At The Darbaar

*"'Venture outside your comfort zone. The rewards are worth it.' –
Rapunzel in Tangled"*

After AA was unceremoniously dropped from the 'people to have faith in' list, we needed another doctor for Sonal because the problem was far from over. In 2010, Sonal's parents then told us about a homoeopath; I will refer to him as BB, who used to practice at a subsidized clinic for the needy as *seva* in the *darbaar* which Sonal's spiritual guru comes to when he is in Mumbai. Sonal's side of the family has tremendous faith in Darbaar Sahib Halani, which was earlier in Sion, and the various gurus, including the latest guru, who is respectfully referred to as Sainjin or Baba Sai. So strong is their faith in him that his blessings are sought whenever they want to start a new venture (business or personal) or journey or task.

Sonal and I were also married off by the same guru, and so were my sister-in-law and her husband. Even if there is an illness in the family, he is spoken to and an assurance sought. Personally met, if he is in Mumbai or spoken to on the phone if he is not. Once a year, my parents-in-law used to make a trip to Ajmer to visit him there and offer their services. I see the same level of reverence in every member of the family and every disciple at the *darbaar*. BB practiced at this *darbaar*. Since there was an element of faith in the guru, more than in BB or his treatment, Sonal was willing to give that a shot. Faith, as they say, works in mysterious ways. Who knows what would work for whom and how if there is faith. Why else do placebos work for some, if not faith? Since Sonal had faith, I was willing to go along with whatever she wanted. Whether faith worked or medicine, allopathy did or homeopathy, or counseling did or medication, was unimportant. Getting better was the primary goal. So, we went to see the homoeopath.

His clinic was in one of the smaller back rooms of the temple. On one side of the room, there were two tiny cabins. One was for the doctor and the other was for the compounders designate who dispensed the doctor prescribed medication. The remaining strip of the room was the waiting area with two low wooden benches for people to sit. They could have seated about eight people tops (ten if you didn't mind having someone's elbow sticking into your gut). Thankfully, there was a window on the wall and an overworked fan overhead. A back door opened into one of the typical narrow by lanes of Mumbai with small houses constructed side by side in a long row.

Inside the clinic, at least twenty people were waiting to see the doctor, with the number swelling rapidly. There were more patients (since it is a subsidized clinic and hence treatment is rather cheap) than space in the waiting room, and people (including us) had spilled over outside the clinic too, in the narrow lane for a breath of fresh air. Sonal feels uncomfortable among large crowds, and in that constricted environment, I couldn't blame her for even I was uncomfortable. Waiting outside was an undesirable option, too, since it meant standing for an indeterminate and uncomfortable period. Since we took Shlok along most times, their inconvenience was unacceptable to me. I was pretty sure Shlok would eventually get bored and ask to be taken home. After all, how long could I hold his interest with his fleeting attention span, showing him the trains that went by?

To add to the wait, since homeopathy requires working at the root cause of every disorder, the diagnosis takes very long, and even here, the time taken by the doctor to deal with each patient hovered around 20-25 minutes for repeat patients and over 40 minutes for new patients. So, the wait was painfully interminable. But since this concerned Sonal's health and the well-being of our familial bonding, I tolerated the bilge.

After a wait that would have greyed a few strands of my hair, by which time, Shlok and I were enormously bored and hungry, it was finally our turn to meet the doctor. With a sigh of relief, we entered his cabin. I saw a formally attired middle-aged, dark, portly, typical Sindhi-looking man sitting in the doctor's chair. That would be BB. Since the doctor knew Sonal's entire family, because of the Baba Sai connection (in fact, my in-laws and the doctor were on first name terms), there were the usual pleasantries. *'How is your father? How is your mother? How is your sister? Where is she now? What is she doing?'*

One peculiarity of the Indian culture is that we refer to even unrelated elders as 'uncle' or 'aunty'. That was the case here too. He wasn't 'doctor' for Sonal. He was 'uncle' to her. Therefore, he was 'uncle' for me too. 'Uncle' didn't seem to be in a hurry. He seemed happy to engage in a verbal equivalent of 'amble rather than trot'. Maybe he wanted to get Sonal to be comfortable before the diagnosis.

Is that one of the reasons why the session with each patient takes so much time, I wondered. Pleasantries dispensed with, he asked for Sonal's complete case history - when it started, what the symptoms were, which doctors had we been to, what medicines Sonal was on and so on and made copious notes. We related the entire story to him. Sonal was also carrying her prescriptions from AA and he took a look at them as well. He kept nodding knowingly in between and also kept referring to a well-used, dog-eared book to nail down each and every symptom described by Sonal during the course of the diagnosis to arrive at the best possible course of treatment for Sonal. Sometimes, he would refer to the book, find a symptom written there and ask if Sonal suffered from the same symptoms. He arrived at a diagnosis at long last, wrote it down, and asked us to wait in the waiting room for the medication.

Three people were surrounded on three sides by dusty cabinets that held hundreds of bottles with medicinal liquid in them. Each bottle had a strip of white medicinal tape stuck on it and the name of the medicine written on the tape in ballpoint pen ink. From the faded writing on the grubby tape that was white no more, it was clear that the bottles had seen better days. I wondered how they were able to even tell one bottle from the other. What if the wrong medication is dispensed by mistake? I only hoped that the right medicine was being given to Sonal.

Sonal had her own reservations with homoeopathic medication because as is commonly known, homeopathy medicines are dispensed in small sugar balls with medicinal liquid poured over them. Sugar! Most people like the medicines because they are small sweet balls that need to be consumed, unlike in allopathy, where the tablets could be either too large, bitter, or both. Kids, in particular seem to be fonder of homoeopathic medicine for this reason. Shlok was also given a small bottle with plain sugar balls (minus any medication) to eat. Sort of like a treat from the doctor's office. He accepted it willingly with a smile and a word of shy thanks for the compounder coterie. But I could see Sonal's face contorting almost in disgust at the sight of so much sugar. Nevertheless, because the medicine was from Baba Sai's clinic, with his implied blessings, she steeled herself to take the medication home and made an earnest attempt to follow the regime.

Sonal was asked to return after a fortnight. For that fortnight, whatever was in our power (including prayer), we did. Even though these medicines were sweet, Sonal very sweetly and uncomplainingly, completed her course.

To no avail, though. There was no improvement in her condition at all. I hoped that it was because of the oft-repeated homeopathy aphorism that homeopathy took time to take effect but was a permanent cure. I hoped. A fortnight later, when we met the doctor he seemed pretty confident. He was sure that Sonal would be feeling better by then. He asked Sonal how she felt.

Sonal wasn't feeling any different, and she tersely said so. This puzzled the doctor. He was in utter disbelief. He pulled out his notes and pulled out his dog-eared book of spells. He cross-checked and cross-verified his diagnosis again and again. He seemed satisfied that the course of treatment that he had prescribed was correct. But it hadn't worked. So, he seemed to be in a quandary. He didn't know what to do. He kept saying, '*How is it that there is no effect? It should have worked by now. At least some change should have been visible*'.

I was distraught and knew yet again that we would be scouting for another doctor very soon.

As for Sonal, she was not even thinking that far. What had upset Sonal the most in this visit, which was a larger reason not to ever go to BB again was more here and now. Even in the doctor's cabin on the wall behind where the visitor's chair was, she saw a long line of large black ants on the wall. Did I mention that it doesn't matter to Sonal whether the ants are black or red or any other color? That it doesn't matter whether the ants bite or they don't? That it also doesn't matter whether the ants are large or small? Whichever form they are in, they are feared because they are ants. Not for what they can do or for how they look but for what they are.

There they were in the doctor's cabin now. For the doctor, (as for you or me), it wasn't an issue that needed attention. If doctors had to pander to every patient's whims and redesign their cabins accordingly, they would never get any doctoring done at all. But to Sonal, it was nothing but lack of hygiene. It was blasphemy! The uncanny way in which Sonal can track ants anywhere (almost like an anteater, except that she wasn't eating them) always left me dumbstruck.

Sonal's eyes were always skinned to spot the enemy and when she saw them there, in an instant, she lost all hope of any relief coming from the *darbaar*, Baba Sai or no Baba Sai. Her faith in the doctor was eclipsed by the terror lurking in the room. She consoled herself to understand that just because the clinic was in the Baba Sai's *darbaar*, it did not guarantee a cure or even temporary relief.

I had a long discussion with her that started with an attempt to make her understand that it wasn't enough reason to drop the doctor. The discussion became an argument and the argument became a full-blown shouting match. I accused Sonal of not wanting to focus on her recovery and she accused me of not wanting to understand her plight. In retrospect, I know both of us were right. She was indeed making a mistake by running away from her fears. On my part, I was making a mistake too, by not being empathetic and trying to 'win' the discussion. In the end though, her fear won over my frustration and I grudgingly agreed to look for another doctor. So, we dumped BB too. Thumbs down, once again.

CHAPTER IX

Vacation In Tarkarli

*"'Never let the fear of striking out keep you from playing the game!'
- A Cinderella Story"*

Since our relationship had started deteriorating, I thought it was necessary for us to try and grab a few happy moments if we could, at least for Shlok. That would also be one way of relieving Sonal's stress and offering her a few moments of respite from her slavish existence, and perhaps, repair our relationship to some extent. But after her condition started worsening, I was also always cagey about randomly involving her with my friends. Yes, I could tell some of my friends about her disorder and expect at least a couple to understand and compromise with the situation. But that would mean not doing so many things in her presence that were likely to trouble her, like ordering sweets. That seemed a tad too much to expect from anyone. But I couldn't just exclude her from my outings with friends either. I realized I would just have to be selective about what to tell and to whom.

So, when an opportunity presented itself to set aside the banality of our lives for a weekend and go for a short picnic to Tarkarli, along with a few friends and their families, I, in equal parts hesitatingly and eagerly, checked with Sonal. I pre-warned her that if she did agree to go, we would probably be staying in small shacks in a tiny village, and the facilities would not be anything to write home about. Plus, a small village near the sea meant a lot of tree cover, wild shrubbery, *kachcha* roads, and loose sand, which meant there could be anthills by the hundreds and ants by the millions. I tried to present as bleak a picture as I could so that she would go into it with her eyes open if she did.

On one of my work trips, once in San Francisco, I had gone to the supermarket to pick up a loaf of bread. There, on the door of a doughnut display, I read a handwritten notice which had all manner of warnings. About there being milk in them and hence lactose intolerant people should stay away. About there being sugar in them so diabetics should stay away. About gluten, yeast, etc. For a moment, I thought how noble it was of them to warn everyone, even at the expense of their wares not getting sold. But eventually, it dawned on me that they were protecting their own hide, lest they be sued by someone who buys it and gets sick on its account. The US being what it is, it is more likely than not that a miss like that would result in a lawsuit.

I had similar thoughts about presenting all manner of warnings to Sonal, which I did. Not that I thought Sonal would sue me for not letting her know about everything in advance, but still, that is how I was with Sonal. As much to protect myself from backlash later as to protect her from stress on a picnic. But Sonal has often managed to bewilder me with her grit. She did so this time too - by agreeing with remarkable alacrity to go for the trip despite all odds. Readily, and in defiance of all warnings.

Given that we would be a good twelve hours by bus away from Mumbai, in a village that didn't have an airport or wouldn't have enough emergency psychiatric facilities, I was almost terrified that she agreed to go. I didn't know whether to laud her efforts for having agreed or take the safer option of dissuading her and indirectly pushing her further away from recovery, and risk her censure for having asked her at all to begin with. What if she had a panic attack that I was unable to handle when we were there? What if she created an unwitting scene in her panic? How would my friends feel? What would they think? Would they be able to help? Was it a wise thing to do at all? This decision-making was like walking a tightrope, and I wasn't sure which way I wanted to lean.

In the end, however, we decided to do what better sense seemed to prohibit and go ahead with this jaunt. I was almost tremulous with excitement. The temptation for me was snorkelling, which I wanted to try out and was hitherto rueful about the larger possibility of having to miss it. In addition, unwinding with friends, scrounging some respite from the drudgery of everyday routine, holidaying in a rustic setting (something which I dearly love), and good sea food (one of my biggest weaknesses) were things that weighed heavily in favor of the trip. For Shlok, who was still too small, it was another holiday by the beach along with kids of his age for company, and he was excited too. For Sonal, it was a picnic, yes. But it was also another battle. Another obstacle course to complete. Another test of her mettle. *Challenge accepted*, her resolve seemed to say.

It was an overnight journey to Tarkarli. All of us assembled at Andheri Western Express Highway at 8 PM, a motley crew of ten adults and four kids. My friends had their wives and kids along and Shlok was sorted with the three kids there, two girls and one boy. Sonal seemed to be doing alright with my friends' wives, and that was also fine. But I was apprehensive of some foreboding possibility of impending doom. I had a range of thoughts plaguing me, all pessimistic. Until the very end, I wasn't sure if we were making the right decision. The bus was late, and already Sonal seemed to be edgy. That added to my uncertainty about the wisdom of embarking upon this foolish adventure. I prayed with bated breath for things to be alright.

When the bus finally came, we all boarded and gave the driver a piece of our mind for a little peace of mind. The driver looked like a ruffian out of a South Indian movie, with a potbelly, uncut curly hair and a thick moustache, and I expected him to say something like 'yenna rascala, mind it'. To his credit, he wasn't belligerent but sure as hell he wasn't apologetic either. He decided that he wanted to catch up on lost time, and so he unilaterally decided not to stop at the customary halts, much to the passengers' chagrin, who wanted to eat and also use the washroom. After a quick war of words with the South Indian villain, which I was also a part of since Sonal was one of the suffering women, the bus finally halted at a dhaba.

Everyone quickly used the washroom and had a hasty dinner. I was in an unenviable position of walking on eggshells and having to hurry Sonal up, who doesn't like to be rushed, pushed, or forced to do anything. Not that this had anything to do with Sonal's OCD but anything that caused stress was unwelcome since Sonal was prone to attributing everything bad to the failure of the trip. After that, we all slept off, which was a good thing. When we reached the place in the morning, I desperately wished for Murphy to take a break. Let the place where we are staying not be as bad as the bus journey, I thought. I already had a ready-to-explode wife on my hand and wanted to avoid any other stimulus that would set the timer off and blow the bomb.

But! When we reached the place where we had our stay arranged (a series of small rooms owned by a family, practically in the middle of wilderness but by the sea-side), I was aghast to see the number of big red ants there. Not only was there a thick line of ants in our room but the entire place (the veranda, the passage, the benches outside) had millions of ants too. I am not exaggerating. Literally millions. All over the bloody place. My heart sank to new depths I didn't know existed, because I was expecting Sonal to tell me anytime that she would not want to stay in that place and that we should head back. I had already started planning what I would tell my friends. I had already started planning how we would head back. Would we get a bus? Would we have to take a train? I was dreading the prospect of

Sonal expressing an opinion and issuing a diktat.

But hey! Wonder of wonders! My gritty and unpredictable wife surprised me yet again. She resolutely said she would make do. I was so proud of her. Other than exchanging our room with a friend (whose room was slightly smaller but didn't have any ants), there was not even a whimper or whine from Sonal. I was surely not about to ask her – but what about the millions of ants outside? What about the conversation I have already planned with my friends? What about all of that? The frantic pirouetting of my heart subsided and I felt a weight off my chest. I finally began to breathe.

That weekend was a test. Of Sonal's ability to manage herself in a social setting. Of her ability to not crumble to pieces at the sight of ants. To not create a scene through her hysterics. I admit she handled it beautifully. When we had company, she was the epitome of self-control. Not once did she let anyone know how much being there was troubling her. Not one errant squeak. She put on a brave face and made a supreme effort to enjoy with us as much as her dastardly OCD would allow her to. Not just when we were staying in the sub-optimal room but also when local travel was to be undertaken.

Since the location where we were to snorkel was a little far away from where we were staying, the property owners arranged transportation for us. What do you think it was? The back of a dilapidated truck with grungy, grimy, unwashed floorboards. Once again, for everyone else it was an adventure and hence exciting to travel in such a rustic fashion but for Sonal, it was a huge task.

I was tired enough to have heard her complain in the privacy of our room because, well, she did complain. Sonal was back then at a point where one line of ants was enough to make her want to give up on her doctor, who had Baba Sai's blessings. This was far more than just one line. In the middle of a picnic too. How was she to enjoy it? How would she let me enjoy it too?

In retrospect, I know how difficult it would have been for her to manage all that but back then I was getting irritated with her constant poppycock about the surviving conditions not being up to her imperial levels of satisfaction. I don't rightly remember what I said but I can safely say I would have snubbed her and browbeaten her into a submissive silence.

When we reached the snorkelling point, I had to once again convince her that the water was clean and that the equipment that we were using was clean as well. At long last, after plenteous hesitation (partly out of disgust and partly out of fear), she agreed to snorkel. Sonal, the instructor and I got kitted up and jumped into the water. We went inside the water, and sure enough, after a brief search, we saw amazing specimens of marine life in all their splendor. Small, pretty, colorful sea creatures everywhere. Schools of colorful fish, beautiful tropical plants, coral reefs, the works. What a magnificent experience that was! I was thrilled to bits. To add to it, Sonal managed brilliantly too. I was once again impressed with how well Sonal managed it, all things considered.

After taking our turns, we all headed back in the same bedraggled truck. We were to head back to Mumbai the same day. We reached our rooms, bathed and got ready for a sumptuous lunch of sea food. Then we headed back. The return journey was fairly eventless. Which, believe me when I say it, was a big relief. No ants, good bus, everything. I felt rested and Sonal was also just a trifle more relaxed and cheerful. Good. But vacation over.

Sometimes I liked to pretend that Sonal's OCD was gone. That we have witnessed a miracle. That she is not triggered anymore. That is not terrified of ants anymore. That I don't have to worry about what upsets her and what doesn't anymore. That Shlok has a regular childhood. That Sonal and I have a regular, mundane, boring life. That I have a regular, mundane, boring 9 to 5 job. It was so strange that situations could make a regular, boring, mundane life aspirational. What is boring for one is desirable for another; for me. This was one such time. When we had such a great trip amidst millions of ants, I wished my pretence was a reality. But it was wishful thinking, I knew. Her OCD wasn't going anywhere so soon. My aspiration for a boring life was still a dream. Sigh! Back to the grind.

CHAPTER X

The Intensity Of The Problem – Glimpse II

"You have to accept the storms and the rainy days and the things in life that you sometimes don't want to face.' - Bai Ling"

We were down two doctors (AA and BB) and we did not have any respite yet. We had to find a doctor whom Sonal was comfortable with. We got to know of another psychiatrist, CC. He operated out of a small rented room in a poorly lit and a typical dingy looking nursing home near Andheri railway station. A youngish, simple looking, South Indian chap, he was recommended by Sonal's friend who was battling with depression and therefore, his patient. The doctor belonged to her community and they had things and people in common. Besides, Sonal's friend is a vivacious extroverted woman, and hence she may have clicked with the doctor. But OCD and depression are two completely different animals. CC's treatment may have worked for Sonal's friend but the experience certainly didn't work for Sonal for various reasons.

First, it was a little far away for Sonal. Not as far as it was inconvenient to reach, maybe. It was in a very crowded area with heavy traffic and no parking space. I had to park at quite a distance to reach the clinic. So, Sonal would get off and I would go to find parking and then walk back to the nursing home. She would not like going up alone and waiting for me in the dingy space, and if she had to go there alone, it would tire her.

Second, Sonal was not too kicked about the hygiene levels of the nursing home. It was a gloomy place. There was some carpentry underway too, so the place looked more crowded than ever. The corridor was narrow and there was saw dust all around. One had to step over planks of wood and contend with the noise of drilling or hammering. Over all, it wasn't an environment one would typically visualize when one thinks of visiting a psychiatrist.

Lastly, we faced the same issue there as well, as we did with AA. We recited the OCD rhapsody all over again (it was almost becoming a routine and I was getting good at it). But after a good 20 minutes of talking, during which time, the doctor was nodding his head at erratic, uncoordinated points in time, which appeared a little funny to me, the verdict was as brisk as with AA. The remedy was pretty much the same too. Just medication, no counseling. No empathy, no shoulder to cry on. It was bound to not work and did not work. But we did go to him for a few sessions, to give him a fair chance and not flit from one place to the other indiscriminately. Since the treatment method did not improve and Sonal's condition also didn't seem to be getting any better (in fact, it worsened), we had to stop going to CC as well.

Meanwhile, the cleaning routine had seen another steep spike. By now Sonal would be involved in cleaning the house for close to five hours a day. Every day! To add to that, after dinner, she would sluice the kitchen platform and the walls behind the gas stove with detergent and sweep and mop the entire house to ensure that no food had remained spilled on the floor to serve as an invitation to ants. The entire house, including the bedroom and other far-off corners of the house where there was no chance of any food reaching at all. But in her mind, that needed to be cleaned too, along with the other rooms. I would watch her toil herself to exhaustion and realized it was not healthy. Not just because of her OCD but also because she was physically draining herself of all the energy that she had.

She was losing weight at ominous speeds. Once, just to check just how difficult it was for her to resist the urge to clean, and because I just couldn't believe, regardless of what I had seen, that if she put her mind to it, she wouldn't be able to defy the pull to perform her rituals, when she wanted to sweep the floor, I asked her if she could resist the urge. '*What if I do not give the broom to you? Can you resist it?*'

I took the broom away from her. She tried to resist it for a minute or so. She had a pained expression on her face. She fidgeted uncomfortably, snivelled a bit and when she could control it no more, started crying. '*Please give me the broom. Mujhe bahut takleef ho rahi hai*' (It is troubling me a lot).

She pleaded with so much emotion that it shook me. I felt ice up my spine. Ever watched a horror scene build up in a movie? There is pin drop silence for a few long, tense seconds. Then the sinister music starts and it builds up to a crescendo and you know that a jump scare is imminent. You hold your breath, and then it comes - the jump scare. Even though you know what will happen, it makes you miss a heartbeat. Shakes you to the bone. Until it passes and you know it is just a movie. That's how I felt - minus the music. If there were music, it would have been better. At least it would have meant that this was not real. But it was real, and it was not going to pass in the next scene.

I gave her the broom back and she felt satisfied only after she had completed her rituals. The addict had had her fix and had reached her high. All these experiences were very new and surprising (not to mention shocking) for me too and I had no idea how to deal with them or how to deal with her. We have gone through much worse after that but since these were early days and since these experiences were new, their impact was harder. More scarring. They still give me goose bumps when I think of them. It was disconcerting to say the least that we didn't have a good doctor or counselor to go to, and Sonal's condition kept worsening.

Yes, I did give in to Sonal's demand for the broom when I saw that she was anguished by the thought of not being able to clean, to the point of a break down. But it begets the question of whether everything that a sufferer wants to do should be allowed just because disallowing it would cause more stress. In other disorders, it might very well be the case, but in OCD, I found out through my interaction with doctors and through the literature I read that there can't be a bigger mistake than that. The more one concedes to OCD, the more demanding OCD becomes. Before we woke up to this knowledge, I frequently made the same mistake with Sonal, which obviously led to the worsening of her condition. In the beginning, before I was aware of her condition and what was expected of me, I would let her do everything she wanted to do and would also help her do it just so she would be a little less stressed out and we could have some peace at home. Little did I know then that I was making a huge mistake that we would have to pay for so dearly.

If I had known any better, I would have attempted to strike a balance between what she would be allowed to do and what not. Our journey could have been much smoother, and we would have made far more progress much faster. Neither of us knew what the correct approach was. Both she and I have lost too much time on incorrect approaches because of ignorance about the disorder. Whatever approaches worked for us, which we identified through trial and error, may not have eliminated the problem completely but have still brought a measure of relief to an otherwise seemingly unending misery.

What with Sonal's condition worsening and my inability to deal with it with the maturity required, needless to say, my work had also started getting affected. From a person who was known to be extremely calm and unruffled in the worst of situations, I was turning into a vicious animal and an intemperate worker. I would pick up fights at the drop of a hat and generally make the lives of colleagues and co-workers miserable. Just because my life at home was miserable. It wasn't as if I planned my targets or planned the occasions for losing my temper. Occasions to lose temper just seemed to present themselves to me.

Years back, when I was just a kid, I had to buy a local train ticket on one occasion, and I didn't have the right change. Since I had only a note of a higher denomination, I was already half expecting the ticket seller to give me grief on it. I had decided even as I waited in the queue that I would fight back if he did give me grief. That is precisely what happened. The ticket seller asked for change, and I yelled at him. When I related this incident to my mother, she told me that the fight took place because I was spoiling for one. Because I had it planned. I could have walked away without a fight if I had chosen to. She also told me philosophically that often being congenial achieves far more than being a jerk, a lesson that I embraced.

I understood. Since then, I haven't ever planned a fight. But in office, any small thing was enough to tick me off and shouting matches would ensue. Just because I could. I was a co-founder in the company I worked for and was second only to the CEO. So, I had a lot of say in most things. As a result, I had unwittingly begun to abuse my power. I used to almost bite my colleagues' heads off. Unnecessarily. There were hushed whispers about me that I knew of. A few trusted sub-ordinates also came up to me and asked me,

'Sir, if you don't mind, can we ask you something? Why are you becoming such a monster?'

'Because they deserve it',I said stubbornly.

They slunk away quietly, not wanting to incur my wrath. Now, I realize how much courage it must have taken for them to approach me with such a question, call me a monster to my face and risk my vitriol. Although these were my trusted lieutenants, even they were scared of me. Even if any of them wanted to tell me where I was going wrong, I was just not approachable. My popularity nose-dived, I incurred widespread odium, lost a couple of good friends and perhaps everyone's respect from office because of my sometimes obnoxious and most times puerile behavior.

At times, even mediation was required between some colleague and me over some issue that would crop up because of my intransigent and bullying behavior, and the mediator would have to be my boss since I was answerable to no one else. While my boss was completely on my side in most situations, at least while the issue was being discussed, whenever he got a chance to speak to me alone, he would advise me to settle down and not blow things out of proportion. I would always be defiant and defensive and tell him that I knew what I was doing. I would feel a great deal of resentment towards him for having spoken to me like that. How dare he? But in retrospect, maybe I didn't know what I was doing. No! I definitely didn't. The tone that he would use with me would also be more conciliatory than provocative. But I can see that only now.

I had started feeling road rage too, something that was totally uncharacteristic of me. I would not pick up actual fights with errant drivers and jaywalkers (and that was maybe more because of the fear of getting hurt – I'm not given to juvenile behavior such as picking up fist fights with strangers, thankfully), but I was hurling expletives at them under my breath and honking unnecessarily out of impatience, something I've never done. I usually like to restrict the use of the horn as much as possible. Sometimes, I even play a game with myself. To get through a full day's driving without honking even once. Most times, I win too. On one occasion, Shlok had even commented on it. His five year old observant brain said, '*Nana bahut horn bajaate hain, papa nahi bajaate*' (grandfather uses the horn a lot, papa does not).

But back then, my hand used to be practically glued to the horn. Shlok observed that as well and remarked that not only did I honk more often now, but I would also give the other car a dirty look as I passed it by.

I was also less than an ideal husband. No, I was less than an average husband. I was always spoiling for a fight. Sonal and I started going hammer and tongs over situations that were huge for me from a 'need for adherence to rules 'point of view but meant little or nothing to her. For example, I wanted to have lunch before two in the afternoon on weekends. Or I wanted Shlok to be allowed to go down and play. But these were unimportant for Sonal and wouldn't be followed. That would irritate me.

Or we would fight over situations that were huge for her (from the point of view of performing her rituals) but for me were very trivial. Like, she didn't want me to eat anywhere else other than on the dining table. Or she wanted me to check my shoes every time I entered the house to rule any dirt out. These would be petty for me and her fastidiousness would annoy me. The frequent and often bitter fights led to a chasm being created between us. The OCD monster would be up against the monster in me. I would snap at her at the littlest of things. The sheen of the fissile relationship was eroding and being riven with a crack.

Not surprisingly, Sonal didn't feel too confident about sharing her troubles with me. Perhaps she wondered how I would be able to help anyway. She didn't think that I understood her pain and had alleged it often enough. (That riled me even more). Or maybe she was scared of telling me because she may have thought I would scold her for being so irrational. It was a mix of both. So, our communication faltered. The bonding weakened further. I wish now I had reached out to her then. It would have meant keeping my battered and bruised ego aside and going through a lot more than I thought I was. But I should have done it - to understand what she was going through and to help her deal with her suffering. Maybe strengthen the bond a little. But no. How could I allow my ego to be quashed?

Meanwhile, having already seen the insides of the clinics of three doctors and having been disappointed all three times, we were at our wits' ends trying to figure out whom we should approach, whom we should put our faith in. We were desperate to put Sonal under the care of a good doctor. Sonal needed a psychologist more than a psychiatrist. That was one thing which we were very clear about. At least I was. Sonal needed someone she could talk to, not someone who would treat her like a part of an assembly line - check, prescribe medication, repeat. There was this uncertainty of the future and confusion about the course of action. Our relationship was tempestuous at best. The burnish was all but gone. Sonal's health was at an all time low and only getting worse. Shlok was suffering silently in the process. The glitter and shimmer of living in a happy family was fast dissipating. Life was at its nadir. There just seemed to be no solution in sight. What should we do? What should we try that we already hadn't?

We were so desperate to find a good counselor that we were not past checking the yellow pages for the telephone numbers of counselors. We were completely okay with hunting out a few of them who practiced close to where we stayed, visiting a few of them and then deciding whom we would want to continue her treatment with. Through trial and error. Definitely not an ideal way to look for a mental health professional and entrust Sonal's mental health to them. What if things went wrong? What if the situation worsened? What if? But there seemed to be no other way that I could think of. Sonal had, in any case, left the responsibility of the search, identification and assessment of the shrink to me. I was fishing in a shallow pool, wasn't I? So, looking up the Yellow Pages is exactly what I did.

CHAPTER XI

Looking Up The Yellow Pages

"'You make a choice, commit to it and live with the consequences. Talk is cheap. Doing is hard.' - A Town of Eureka"

We looked up the contact numbers of four different counselors from the yellow pages, and reached out to them one after another. We fixed up meetings with them on four successive days so that the experiences would be fresh and decision making would be easier.

The first counselor we visited (DD) was just a quixotic school counselor who practiced part-time from her house. When we reached her home, she said she had to leave for a function and would not be able to spend too much time with us. This, after having a confirmed appointment with her. She was a short, squat woman with a restless disposition. Not what I would want from a psychologist. My idea of a good psychologist was a calm and soft-spoken person, who inspired some confidence purely by his or her demeanor. DD didn't. I also soon realized from the way she spoke that she wasn't going to be able to help either. Telling her the entire story seemed like dawdling. Just fifteen minutes into the conversation, I wanted out.

But since we had sought her out, we did our bit. Ideally, we would have liked to tell her the entire story, not leaving out anything, although, it was getting arduous to have to recite the same story over and over again to so many people. But in her case, we shortened it. She just made some sympathetic noises, and even to me (who at that point had practically no knowledge on the subject), her suggestions sounded quite amateurish. Nothing substantive. Like when Sonal mentioned that she couldn't control doing certain things excessively, DD shook her head disapprovingly and lamely said, *'You shouldn't do it. Stop doing it'.*

Really? Stop doing it? Those are your pearls of wisdom? I don't mean to sound disrespectful, but she was rather like the next-door neighbor who offers friendly advice to a woman if her husband came home drunk. The one who goes 'tut tut' and makes a disapproving cluck or gesture if something is amiss but is not able to provide constructive, healthy suggestions to get out of the situation. So, she was rejected halfway through the session. Strike one. We left her place pretty disappointed. I was hoping our experience with the other three would not be as bad.

The following day, we had an appointment with the second counselor, EE. She seemed a lot better than DD. She had a clinic tucked away in a corner in a lane that we weren't even aware existed. But at least, it was a clinic. There was, at least, a professional feel to the place. This was not more than five minutes away from our house. But we had to wait awhile because she had stepped out. I glanced at the various posters in her clinic and tried to see if there was anything on OCD. I didn't find anything. Did that mean anything? Stop being foolish, I told myself. If a doctor had to put up something for every disorder he treated on his clinic walls, he'd have a terribly cluttered wall.

After about fifteen minutes of waiting, she walked in. EE was a quiet, swarthy lady, unsmiling but not unpleasant, with sharp eyes. As I also found out after talking to her, an equally sharp brain. We told her the entire story too. In my moments of idle craziness, I have often wished I had recorded Sonal's entire story on my phone and played it for every new doctor we visited. She had a few brilliant ideas up her sleeve about how to handle the obsessions when they struck. In her suffering, Sonal's reasoning had nosedived, and hence, many parallels, analogies, simple tricks, obvious but seemingly crazy methods needed to be thought of and used.

One of EE's suggestions was for Sonal to wrap a taut rubber band around her wrist. *'Every time you get a thought, pull the rubber band back and let it snap back on your wrist.'*

The sting caused by the rubber band would help Sonal distract herself from her intrusive thoughts. Seemed like an idea worthy of trying in theory, but it didn't work on Sonal. Maybe because Sonal wasn't prepared enough for therapy, or maybe because she didn't consider it worth trying. I didn't even see her try. She didn't even wear a band in her hand to try it out. But to me, EE seemed alright. Given enough time, she seemed like she would be able to help Sonal out of her problem. She also didn't seem to be in a hurry to see other patients. She gave enough time to Sonal to unburden herself to her heart's content. That was a positive sign too. So, she was kept on the back burner. To be chosen or rejected based on the experiences with the other two counselors. We came home fairly satisfied with our experience.

The next evening, we had an appointment with the third counselor. It took us a bit to locate her place, and we were delayed by ten minutes. Since I have this obsession (or maybe the wrong word, let's call it fetish) of reaching on time, I was asking Sonal to hurry up, and she was getting irritated because she couldn't 'just leave,' and I was making her life miserable about that. Finally, when we reached our destination, I calmed myself down that a ten minute-delay was not so bad. But the experience with the third counselor, FF, did not start off well. The counselor herself reached for the appointment very late, and Sonal was getting antsy (pardon the pun). She was irritated with me now for having rushed her and for having given her grief over being late.

This, incidentally, was the story of my life most times. While I would be ready on time, Sonal would take forever, which would irritate me. I would pester her about that, and we would argue. Often when we reached our destination, whomever we were meeting would be late. Then it would be Sonal's turn to scowl. It had happened before, and it happened at FF's clinic as well.

We had had to bring Shlok too since we couldn't keep him anywhere else. The poor little boy was sleepy. We made him sleep on the couch in the waiting room while we waited. Shlok did not know of any other type of existence but it felt terrible to make him go through these things. He ought to have been home, sleeping in a comfortable bed, not on a couch in a strange place. The sub-optimality of the parenting that we were giving Shlok struck me hard at all such moments. But there was nothing I could do about it.

Sonal was also tired and was getting more and more chafed by the minute. She just wanted to get done with it and reach home. I was beginning to worry. I didn't want Sonal to lose patience and walk out without meeting the counselor. Or to form an incorrect opinion based on just the counselor's tardiness, which could very well have been an exception. In those days, I found every moment a challenge. There was always something unsolved, some new mind numbing obstacle to cross. If my life of back then were to be made into a video game, it would easily be one of the toughest ones to play. I didn't want to play this game but nobody asked me. So, I was playing it. I was praying for FF to come soon. Finally, after a delay of thirty minutes, a smart, Maharashtrian lady, entered the clinic briskly. She smiled, apologized to us for making us wait and invited us inside her cabin.

The entire story was parroted again. Each time, there was more to add since we were also including details of the treatment until then. She heard us patiently. She also seemed to be knowledgeable. One of her suggestions to Sonal was to keep a comb with sharp teeth in her hand. Whenever the obsessions struck her, she would have to clench the comb in her palm so that the sting caused by the teeth of the comb would help her distract herself. I thought it was yet another brilliant idea that could work. It was similar to the rubber band idea, but it was equally brilliant for its simplicity. Once again, we left the place with some hope. We now felt that we would indeed be able to find someone good enough to suit Sonal's needs and help her get better. I was feeling lighter because in two days we had found two different people who seemed to be good.

Both the rubber band and the comb tricks had high potential to make Sonal feel better, but they didn't. The reason I surmised back then was only poor follow-through by Sonal. She would just cave in halfway. Or not even try. But I know better now. These things didn't work with Sonal because they weren't strong enough counters to drag her away from her obsessive thoughts. They were also not structured well-enough. So, FF was put on the back burner too, along with EE since we had one more person to meet.

But the apparent similarity in the two approaches by EE and FF and the slight difference in the vehicle used just show how, inexact and multi-variable fraught a science, psychology is. Different psychologists might have different approaches, different tricks, different illustrations and examples all aiming to solve the same problem in the same person. Here, two counselors suggested two different methods, both of which sounded logical and exceedingly simple to execute and aimed to resolve the same problem, but neither worked for Sonal.

That is not to say that a third approach, similar in intent but different in nature, would not work. That is also not to say that these approaches would not work on anyone else. It depends upon so many variables like the skill of the counselor, the confidence he or she is able to inspire in the sufferer, the rapport between the counselor and the sufferer, the motivation to improve provided by the counselor to the sufferer, the will to change exhibited by the sufferer and so on and so forth. It all seems like a finely balanced chemical equation, requiring various chemicals in exact proportions to work. A little off and it may not work. Or worse, backfire.

The last counselor, GG - a male this time, had a clinic in Bandra. The clinic was undergoing renovation, and we were sitting in a makeshift consulting room with old, rickety furniture. GG, a portly, moustachioed gentleman in his fifties with dyed hair, apologized to us for the mess and began the session. It seemed to me that the incidence of our sessions beginning with the counselor apologizing to us was rising. First DD, then

EE, then FF and now GG. Sonal was once again running a new counselor through her story.

As misfortune would have it, a few minutes into the session with GG, an ant crawled onto the table, right in front of Sonal while GG was talking to her. GG got a firsthand experience right then of how debilitating it was for Sonal to see ants because once again, Sonal couldn't tolerate the presence of ants moving about so freely in her presence. She was first distracted and wasn't listening to GG. Then when the anxiety was too much for her to bear, she started crying.

The experience shook GG a little too, because he seemed flustered, defensive and even more apologetic. He picked up the ant and discarded it. I put my arm around Sonal and tried to soothe her. It took a little effort to get her to stop crying and assuring her that there were no more ants around. She did stop crying, and yet again, it struck me how very child-like Sonal had become.

After understanding Sonal's condition, GG suggested that a few basic tests be done on Sonal. Tests like the Rorschach and Thematic Apperception Test. Today, I know how irrelevant and unnecessary these tests were for Sonal's condition, but back then, this seemed like a very professional way to approach things to us neophytes, given our lack of knowledge. Also, this was something that neither EE nor FF had suggested. He also stated that if there was any medication required, he would recommend a good psychiatrist to us.

Lastly, he also turned out to be my mother's distant cousin. His surname was the same as my mother's maiden surname, and I asked him if he knew any of my maternal relatives. You bet he did. So, he was my uncle. He had apparently also come for my wedding. So, I was hoping for, if not preferential treatment, at least the best possible. That, coupled with his seemingly knowledgeable air, decided for us that he would be the one we would put our faith in all over again. Although he was a trifle expensive too, compared to the others we had met. So, EE and FF went out of the window, and GG was our new messiah, the coxswain who would ferry us out of the bog to a life of freedom and happiness. We hoped.

When we got home after visiting GG, I asked Sonal,

'Why are you so scared of ants? Kya ho jaega agar ants aa gaeen to?'(What will happen if there are ants around?).

She: *'I don't know.'*

Me: *'Do you think you cannot handle the ants?'*

She: *'I know I can.'*

Me: *'Then? Why do you fear them so much?'*

She: *'I don't know.'*

Me: *'Sonal, you need to know. If I am scared of snakes because I think they are poisonous, I shouldn't be scared if I know that the poison has been removed. For me to not be scared of them, I need to know why I am scared of them, to begin with. Not knowing why you are scared of ants makes it difficult to tackle the problem.'*

She: *'I don't know'.*

Me: *'You must try and find out.'*

She: *'Okay.'*

GG called us to a clinic in Andheri, which was another nursing home that he practiced out of. That place has a psychiatric stay-in facility too, which had a door that was locked from the outside. It was one made of iron bars. One of the attendants had to unlock the door whenever anyone wanted to go in or come out. It looked awfully imposing and restrictive. Was it that the patients admitted there were so far gone that they had to be locked up so that they didn't try to escape? I often wondered. I am pretty sure that thought would have crossed Sonal's mind too. Possibly, that is also the reason why she always resisted getting admitted to a mental hospital to deal with her problem. Maybe social stigma too. She may be thinking about what others would say. That Sonal was admitted to a mental hospital? Was Sonal going mad? Those thoughts are enough to make the option of getting admitted undesirable for anyone, even at the cost of the condition worsening.

Months later, when Sonal's condition worsened, she wanted to be free of the routine responsibilities of taking care of the house and Shlok and me. She had said that she would be able to focus on her therapy only if she were not burdened with other responsibilities. That is when the doctors had suggested admission. Their opinion was that if she were admitted, there would be a posse of doctors to take care of her, and she would also not be burdened with other responsibilities. That would not leave her with any excuse not to do her therapy, which would definitely help.

She had vehemently refused to get admitted, despite knowing the benefits of such a move fully. Maybe because of what she had seen in this place. Nobody would like to be cooped up in such a constraining environment, with little or no freedom. Particularly a person like Sonal, who was in full possession of her faculties apart from this one anomaly.

It is also true that the environment sometimes contributes to worsening the condition. A mildly sick person may start feeling worse if admitted to the hospital in the presence of other patients, doctors, nurses and medical paraphernalia. Sonal didn't want that to happen to her. She would say she would go mad if she were admitted to the hospital.

It was in such a disquieting kind of place that her psychological fitness tests were conducted. There was a separate room that looked like a classroom with lots of desks and benches neatly aligned in two columns, with a whiteboard on the wall. The test sheets were given by a twenty-something girl who discreetly sat a few desks away. However, Shlok and I were allowed to sit on the same desk as Sonal with the simple caveat – that I wouldn't help Sonal (or rather, influence her answers with my feelings). Sonal reluctantly but diligently went through the inkblot and Thematic Apperception Test. Then she was made to go through another test that required her to draw certain things and people. This caused all three of us to snigger because of Sonal's poor drawing skills. She drew misshapen people and objects and while I am no one to judge since I draw poorly myself, both Shlok and I still made fun of Sonal and got her to laugh too. A moment of levity in a sombre episode. Comic relief, so to speak.

Lastly, she was given one multiple-choice objective test, which had 500 + questions, which I now know was MMPI. This test we took home for Sonal to finish at leisure. Put us back by a tidy sum, those tests. But money was the least of our concerns then. Sometime during the week, Sonal finished the test, and I went back to submit it. A week later, the results were declared. We had an appointment with GG where we were to know what the tests said. I haven't been so apprehensive of any of my test results at school, as I was this time. What would we get to know?

Since I wanted to trust the man (more out of desperation than out of real understanding of his capabilities), I did not question his verdict that Sonal was suffering from depression and that all the other symptoms of OCD were because of the depression. He stated that once the depression was taken care of, the OCD would take care of itself. In one corner of my mind, there was some irresolution. If two psychiatrists had diagnosed this to be OCD, how could GG call it just depression? If the others thought OCD was dominant, how was GG calling it a secondary issue? Seemed too simple to be true. Was I making a mistake in trusting a psychologist over two psychiatrists?

But in another corner of my heart, I was secretly glad too. Depression seemed so much easier to deal with than OCD. I also thought there would be fewer questions. People would have at least heard about it and would not be sceptical. They would not brand my wife as insane. It could perhaps be eliminated with counseling alone, I hoped. GG seemed fairly confident of being able to deal with it. So be it, I said. Let's roll with the treatment (read counseling) to fight depression. I know now that it was nothing but wishful thinking on my part, willing him to be correct. I wish I hadn't.

GG suggested that we visit a psychiatrist and re-evaluate the medication that Sonal was on, since we were not going to CC anymore. Psychiatrist? This was a dampener. I thought there wouldn't be one required anymore. But I didn't let it show lest Sonal get disillusioned about the whole idea. It was a task to keep her motivated about her treatment, and I wasn't about to let these things come in the way of her desire to get better. GG put us on to a psychiatrist, HH. We visited HH, who practiced in a small room in one of the nursing homes around our house. Despite her smiling disposition, she seemed a little overbearing and nearly peremptory from the very first meeting. I was hoping Sonal would not have a problem with it. But she saw it and she did have a problem, even though it was not spoken about. At least not in the beginning. In the first meeting, like in every other first meeting, we-narrated-the-whole-goddamned-story-all-over-again.

When I mentioned GG in my narrative, she ignored it once. The second time, with a smile but with ice in her eyes that all but crept into her voice as well, she said – *'Never mind what you told him. Tell me again.'*

Brrr! Ok, ma'am, yes ma'am. So, because of her almost imperious behavior, Sonal didn't take too favorably to HH, which told on her treatment as well. She would go to her reluctantly when she did. Most times, she would reach late. Sonal had lost the ability to manage time well and would almost always arrive late for any appointment. This would make HH haughtier and she would show her disapproval. Sonal didn't like that. So, thereafter, sometimes, when she was getting late, Sonal would just avoid going to her. *'Thoda bhi late jaao to gussa karti hai'* (Even if you reach slightly late, she scolds).

This was self-defeating, and I once again reminded Sonal of the mantra that faith in the doctor is a must. I would ask her to be on time. Sometimes Sonal would say she would try. At other times, she would raise her hands in despair and say she wouldn't be able to do it. That would frustrate me, and sometimes over that too, we would end up fighting. Thus, we trudged along.

So, HH would prescribe the medication required, and GG would talk and talk more to Sonal. I would accompany Sonal for all her sessions (at least with GG), and so would Shlok. For all the sessions, he would call us both inside. Shlok would be sitting there, privy to all the discussions, which I am not sure he should have been exposed to. But he was. I was only hoping Shlok would learn something out of it rather than be damaged. But GG's counseling increasingly began to seem superficial like that school counselor we had visited. I gave him credence for the tests that he had conducted and often thought that I could do a good job of being a psychologist too if I knew how to conduct those tests and if I were authorized to. Prophetic thought, in retrospect.

But for the first time in a very long time, Sonal felt a little better because someone was letting her do what she had wanted to do all along, which is talk. She began to be a little cheerful, although her rituals had not reduced. HH's medication was continuing on track too. After two months of counseling, which was at a frequency of one session (or sometimes two) per week, GG suggested a second round of tests to assess progress. Sonal went through a battery of tests again. Once again in the same class room.

It was monsoon season, and while she was filling in her tests inside, I was outside, showing Shlok some snails and earthworms that had come out of the soil in the flora around that place. I felt that Shlok should not be deprived of the wonders of childhood. His exploratory instincts should not be curbed, and his interests should be allowed to develop well. Even if they were at odds with Sonal's style (or rather her forced method of existence). I tried to expose him to whatever I could so that he could absorb as much information as his sponge-like brain could and then form his own interests rather than do what his mother thinks is best for him (or for her). When I could, I also let him indulge in activities that would dirty his clothes, including playing in the garden, getting wet in the rains, going to the beach, and enjoying the sea (albeit dirty).

I used to climb trees, scale walls, play in puddles, and play in the rain as a kid, and I had a whale of a time back then. It also made me very agile, and brave. I had a wonderful childhood (both enjoyable and educational), and I hoped I would be able to provide the same to Shlok despite his mother's condition and obvious reluctance. So, I made an effort, given the constraints we were living under.

Once again, one week after the tests, the results were out, and they were encouraging. They showed a marginal decrease in Sonal's levels of depression. Splendid news! I hadn't expected a major change, although I could see that Sonal was happier because I was learning to quickly become a pessimist. I used to possess boundless optimism, which then started turning into what I began to euphemistically call realism but in truth, was pessimism. But this news was good. For once, I began to think we had made the right decision. I kept thinking what a stroke of luck it was. How providential to find such a good counselor. From the yellow pages at that. All my apprehensions vanished. All my hopes of soon being rid of Sonal's problems resurfaced. All my doubts about OCD not being secondary and depression not being dominant, as GG had suggested, began to melt away. I was ecstatic.

We celebrated the day by eating out. Just a word on our celebrations is in order here. We were the only family I know whose celebration did not include sweets, chocolates and flowers. If I wanted to woo my wife for Valentine's Day or for our wedding anniversary, I could give her neither chocolates, nor flowers. If we had had a fight and I wanted to make up, I couldn't give her any of these either. If it was a festival and we wanted to celebrate, we couldn't get sweets home. All we used to do for any of these occasions is go for dinner (minus dessert).

We continued the counseling sessions for two more months with GG with renewed vigor. Sadly, the progress stagnated after a point, and no amount of talking and counseling by GG seemed to show any real results. Except that Sonal continued to be slightly happier than she used to be earlier. That, at that time, was a big milestone for us because she had almost forgotten to smile, and the atmosphere at home was depressing when it was not vicious. So, on the one hand, the symptoms didn't seem to have abated even a tiny bit but on the other, Sonal was a shade happier. So, Once again, I was confused about whether the counseling by GG was effective or had become otiose.

Now that I think about it, I wonder how much of the progress was because of GG's counseling and how much of it was actually because of HH's medicines. Couldn't it have been just that the medicines would have spiked her brain's happy chemicals (serotonin), causing her to become cheerful? And that we were wrongly attributing it to GG's counseling? Or was I being unfair to GG?

After about six odd months of counseling under GG, we conducted a third round of tests. This was upon my suggestion. Because I wanted to now check definitively if there really was any point continuing with GG. I didn't want to waste time if it wasn't helping. I certainly didn't want the situation to worsen. So, if it meant that we would have to drop GG and find someone else, I would do that. Sadly, as expected, the situation seemed to have slightly worsened. Sonal had begun regressing. It seemed to me that we had crossed the Big Bang and the Steady State and were now entering the Big Crunch phase. Sigh! Come on, Universe. This can't be happening.

My hopes were dashed, and so was my confidence in the man. We had reached a dead end again, and we were once again unsure of our next steps. GG didn't want to admit it, but he was clearly not yielding the results he expected. His treatment was not working; his claims were ringing hollow. I didn't want Sonal to be used like a guinea pig where people were just experimenting on her. God alone knows how much we had suffered without continuing to have to live in a state of uncertainty all the time. So, we didn't see any sense in continuing with him. Where I used to look forward to Sonal's sessions with him in the hope that she would come out a better person after each session, I had begun to consider it a drudgery that needed to be followed, without expecting any tangible or visible benefits out of the exercise. My quest for identifying a new and better counselor began all over again so that we could move on from GG. I liked it lesser and lesser each time we had to move from one doctor to another. It can't be good for Sonal, I thought. After all, the bread won't cook if you keep opening the oven. But we seemed to be starved for choice. What could we do after all?

CHAPTER XII

Shlok's Compromises

"'It is not our abilities that show what we truly are... it is our choices.'
- Albus Dumbledore in Harry Potter and the Chamber of Secrets"

Life at home, in the meantime, kept oscillating between bad and good. Some bad things were improving, and some good things were getting worse. Shlok had also gotten used to the unnatural lifestyle he had been forced into. Perhaps he melded into it because he wasn't aware of any other type of existence. This is the only life that he has seen, and he does not have an alternate frame of reference to compare his situation with. His situation reminded me of a true story I had read in Readers' Digest years back.

It was about a girl who suffered from some infection in her chest. Her sputum was so tenacious that her back had to be thumped routinely to expectorate it. It was a painful procedure for her, and she would cry out in pain when it happened. But she wasn't aware of any other type of existence, and when she played with her dolls, she would pretend to be a doctor and do the same to her dolls. For her, that was normal. At some point, would she have asked God why it was required to live such a painful life? Or, when she had grown older, would she have questioned God on why she had been singled out for such suffering?

As for Shlok, this was how his life was too. A life full of compromises, of quashing his desires, of a deficit of all things sweet in his life. He could not talk about chocolates and *mithais* at home because that would stress mamma out. He would rarely be allowed to eat anything sweet (even outside the house), at least in the presence of his mother, because that would also stress mamma out. When he did eat anything sweet when he went out with me once in a while, Sonal would want to know what he had eaten so that she could stress herself out because of it. Shlok had started feeling guilty about eating anything sweet even when his mother was not present and had reduced his consumption of sweets.

He was also discouraged from going down to the garden to play. He had a few friends but he couldn't play with them. Sonal's fear about his going to the garden to play was that ants that would climb onto his shoes in the garden would come home. He got used to that compromise as well and would play at home. All on his own, because neither would his mamma allow him to go down, nor would she have the time to play with him, being so consumed in her own suffering. Those few months of Shlok's near-solitary confinement still trouble me sometimes, for my inability to provide him with an ideal environment to grow up.

He was once allowed to have an ice cream on a rare occasion. After a few licks, he accidentally spilled a drop on his tee. Children do that, don't they? Sometimes, elders do it too. Who really has control over a stray drop of melted ice cream making its way down silently from an overflowing cone onto one's hand or clothes? Particularly in the hands of a child, whose speed of eating the ice cream is no match for the speed of the ice cream melting. So, he spilled a drop on his tee. After that no matter how much I tried to convince him that it was alright, he just couldn't enjoy the rest of the ice cream. He knew that his mamma would be stressed and angry. The fear of the repercussion eclipsed the joy of the rare treat, and he started crying. I had to calm him down and tell him that it was alright. Mamma wouldn't see, or if she did, she wouldn't mind.

I knew Sonal would notice though, and she did notice. She did make an issue out of it and yell at the hapless boy, and worsen his already bad trip. Making him feel guilty as hell. Sonal's anxiety did not allow her to let it pass and she had to give in. My irritation at the pettiness of the issue did not allow me to let it pass and I tried to defend Shlok. Sonal and I ended up fighting again. All because a six-year-old had a normal ice-cream spilling episode.

If one sits back and thinks, whose fault was it anyway that we ended up fighting? I refuse to concede that it was Shlok's fault for having spilled one measly drop on his clothes. I also fully understand that Sonal's ire was not her own but was brought about by her inability to deal with her OCD. I suppose, in the end, if there was a fault, it was mine for not having understood Sonal's point of view and for having yelled at her when things could perhaps have been handled more reasonably.

Of all the challenges that Shlok had to face and of all the changes that he had to make in his lifestyle to accommodate his mother, perhaps the most difficult one for him would have been the loneliness. That of being an only child. Of being confined at home. Of not even having his mother play with him. On more than one occasion, he had expressed desire to have a younger sibling. *'I wish I had a baby brother.'* It was my painful duty to reason with him and explain why it was impossible given mamma's condition. Lying to him came easy, given his age. I told him, '*God will not give mamma another baby until she is better.*'

The explanation was simple and in his simple brain made perfect sense, and he bought it. The matter was handled for then. But it was awful to deprive him of company. '*So, if not a sibling, can I have a pet dog?*'

Sonal would never agree to a dog in a million years, OCD or no OCD. First, she is mortally scared of dogs. Then, imagine cleaning up and picking up after the dog. Worse, if it is not toilet trained, which most dogs aren't, in the beginning. Plus the food that would spill. Sonal was pretty certain there would be ants. Not to mention the hair shedding, the vaccinations, the visits to the vet and the smell. It all seemed like too much work to Sonal, who was tiring of her routine responsibilities of taking care of Shlok and the house itself. If the dog was at home, all these responsibilities would be hers to handle. So, it wasn't a good idea, and Sonal was not ready for it. So, I told Shlok, '*Dogs are not potty trained. Since papa will be in office and mamma is not in a position right now, who will clean up after the dog?*'

He didn't want to do it, and this would put him off the thought for a few days. But every once in a while, loneliness would hit him, and he would ask about it again.

I thought that the matter was handled and that he would not bring it up again ever. So, I had a lump in my throat when one day Shlok resignedly said he agreed to clean up after the dog if he was allowed to keep one. He would take care of the dog, feed it and handle the cleaning. It made me cry then. It makes me cry now. Even as I read this while editing, I feel my eyes moistening. Because a small child agreed to take up a task that was repulsive to him just so he could have some company. How lonely do you think he must have felt at that time? I don't remember what I told him then. I must have told him that I would talk to mamma, and we would figure out how and when. But I cried again that night. That one moment highlighted his loneliness like nothing else and made me realize that Shlok was having less than the finest childhood because his parents were less than the finest.

For him to also be exposed to terms like stress, therapy, obsession, compulsion at that age when in school he was just moving to simple five-letter words caused him to mature far faster than kids his age would in some ways. The child learnt far more about 'real life' than kids his age needed to be exposed to. He realized way too early in life that life is not always a fairy tale or a hunky dory affair. He knew where mamma's medicines were kept and which one to give her when she was panicking. He would rush to the kitchen to get mamma a glass of water so that she could take her medicines.

In some other ways, being deprived of day-to-day experiences and small joys caused him to long for certain things that other kids his age would perhaps have outgrown. He continued to remain childlike in those areas. Like longing to play in the rain, the garden, or any other place which was a no-no. Like, longing to eat sweets without apprehension. What a paradox it was - to grow up in some areas faster than others, and remain more a child in others.

He learnt about a lot of things that he could not do. Some through observation, some through experience. Some willingly, some unwillingly. Some at once, some after a series of rebukes from Sonal. He learnt that asking for anything sweet or mentioning anything sweet in front of Sonal was off-limits. Sonal would get mighty stressed at the mere mention of something sweet. Shlok had too often seen Sonal get hysterical, which had taught him well. Even if there was the mention of a sweet in any of Shlok's lessons, he would silently mouth them to me - not say them out aloud. One such Hindi lesson had the word *laddu* in it, and he came to me with a worried look on his face and said,

'*Papa, I cannot show this lesson to mamma. She will get stressed.*'

'*Don't worry, Raja. We will not show it to her,*' I said.

He learnt that just mentioning food when mamma was cleaning was taboo too. Even if he was hungry, he couldn't ask for anything to eat if mamma was cleaning. Like with every other OCD sufferer, Sonal's compulsions were repetitive in nature. If she felt that her routine was disturbed, she needed to do them again. That would happen when food was mentioned while she was cleaning too. Or if someone came to deliver something, she would be disturbed too. He would be screamed at. So, once again, having learnt it the hard way, Shlok chose to go hungry sometimes until mamma finished cleaning rather than risk stressing mamma out and getting upbraided for that. How pathetic was it that a child had to stay hungry and sit quietly until his mamma was satisfied at having completed her rituals! There have been occasions when I have yelled at Sonal for that as well because I couldn't see Shlok having to suffer the way he did.

Sometimes he would come and ask me, '*Papa, when will mamma get better?*'

'*She will, soon.*'

I wouldn't know what else to say. But I didn't believe in it myself. I neither believed that she would get better soon nor did I understand why all this was happening. When was our deliverance scheduled? When would the misery end? In Aleph, Paulo Coelho writes, *'Someday everything will make perfect sense. So, for now, laugh at the confusion, smile through the tears and keep reminding yourself that everything happens for a reason.'*

Yeah, right!

After many efforts at convincing Sonal about the benefits (to Shlok) of having friends and the harmlessness of playing in the building compound, Shlok was finally allowed to go down, and he started playing with his friends. But he learnt that getting friends home was disallowed. Who knew when their shoes had been washed last? Who knew what all would be stuck to their unwashed soles? What if there was something sweet on them? What if they had stepped on something sweet and brought that home? Wouldn't that be an invitation to the ants? Sonal obviously couldn't check Shlok's friends' shoes the way she checked ours. So, the best thing to do was disallow Shlok from bringing his friends home. So, whatever friends he had, they would never come home. It naturally followed that going to his friends' houses was not permitted because if he went to their houses, there would be an obligation to call them to his. So, after having played in the compound for a while, if his friends decided to jam up at one kid's house, Shlok wouldn't join them and would quietly come back home.

He learnt that going to gardens and parks was a strict no-no. So, as long as his friends played on concrete, he would play with them. But when the other kids would go to the garden and play, he would watch them wistfully from outside. Because going into the garden meant being exposed to ants (possibly) that might be lurking in the grass just waiting to climb onto Shlok's shoes. Or fall on his body from trees. It is undeniable that some trees attract ants, and there is a higher likelihood of ants in a garden but not every ant was waiting for Shlok to come, you know.

In the seventies, the Indian film industry produced a blockbuster Hindi movie called *Sholay.* In one of the scenes from the movie, one of the characters who is not in favor of sending her son to the railway station says,

'Nahin station nahin. Wahan rail gaadiyaan aati jaati hain. Mujhe to dar lagta hai.' (No, not the railway station. There are so many trains there; it scares me).

Her husband laughs and says, *'Sab rail gaadiyon ki dushmani hai tumhare sapoot se. Dekhte hi patri chhod kar peechhe lag jaaengi.'* (All trains are your son's enemies. As soon as they see him, they will leave their tracks and run after him).

Sonal and I often had similar conversations. I would ask her why she thought ants would target only Shlok when the others were spared. Her last word would be, '*Why should I risk it?*'

What do you say to that! With such impositions and sanctions in place, I made sure that Shlok always remained top priority for me. I also made sure that he knew that. Sonal would forever stay stressed, and she wouldn't be in a position to offer the child the pampering he would be craving at his age. I gave him all the love that I could. Whenever we went out alone, I also let him indulge himself in as many sweets as he wanted to. Since Sonal was too busy tending to her rituals, I would make extra time for Shlok. I played with him and helped him with his studies and other routine chores. For a while, I had donned the mantle of both the mother and the father. Sonal was in no way capable of taking care of Shlok because she was in no way capable of taking care of her own self. I didn't want to deprive Shlok of the love that he deserved.

Back then, he was old enough to eat and bathe independently but still young enough to enjoy being fed and bathed by me. So, I did that too, on weekends. He would eat half his food, and then when he thought he wanted to get up, he would toy with his food. If I offered to feed him, he would readily agree, and I would feed him. On weekends, he and I would bathe together. I would use some bubble solution and create a lot of bubbles in the bath. We would play with that as if it were snow. He would love to do that. He would also love to ask me to shut my eyes and then throw cold water on me. I would shriek in mock shock; he would shriek in childish glee. These were small things that thankfully were not on the list of 'can't-dos'. So, we would do them as often as I possibly could.

I also talked to him often. *Mano-a-mano.* I could understand him far better than anyone else could. The out-of-context jokes, the mispronounced words, everything. When I was visiting a friend once, her small kids met me and started playing with me in a little while. They pretended to give me something and said, '*Please take temmipees.*'

I asked them twice what they were giving me. '*Temmipees*', they said. I understood only when it was translated by the mother. '*Ten rupees*', she said, beaming. Ah! She told me that a mother knows her child the best and that not even the father knows as much as the mother does. In my case, however, I knew more. I knew all about his friends, his teachers, his favorite subjects, his game preferences, his homework, his doctors, his joys, his fears, etc. Despite being in the state that she was, Sonal also ensured that his studies were not compromised, but she couldn't be there to talk to him as much as he wanted to. So, I tried to fill in the gaps. So, if sometimes he ended up making a statement out of context, as kids are wont to do, I would catch the drift and know what he was talking about while Sonal would not know. We would have to tell her from scratch.

For all the time that Sonal spent on her rituals and for all the preference she showed for her compulsions over Shlok, not for one moment did it seem to me that she did not love Shlok. Let the depiction not make the reader feel that Sonal had become unloving. She doted on Shlok and within the restrictions placed on her by her OCD she would do anything to make him happy. When he was asleep and she would have completed her rituals, she would plant many kisses on his face, sometimes waking him up and annoying him. She would be concerned that he should do well and would speak to me once in a while about his future and his education. Whenever she went shopping, she would inevitably find herself in the children's section in a clothing store and buy clothes for him, perhaps as a way of making up for not being able to give him the time she wanted. She loved him (and still does) 'to the moon and back' and wanted the best for him - so long as it did not interfere with her rituals.

When we had our *tête-à-têtes*, I always let him know that even though life was difficult for him, it didn't mean that mamma didn't love him. It only meant that mamma wasn't able to offer the same liberties to him as other mothers perhaps offered to their children. That it wouldn't last too long. There would soon be a time when he would have the same liberties as any other child. Until then, if he wanted anything he could come and talk to me about it. He would always respond with a statement to the effect that he was alright and that since mamma was unwell, it was required of him to do what he did. '*Chalta hai*', he would say. His '*chalta hai*' would break my heart always. At that age, he had made peace with not receiving a better part of a happy childhood for his mom's sake. It would make me cry. Why did we have to have a child if we were going to deprive him of even the basics?

Much later when things between Sonal and me had deteriorated significantly, there was a time when Shlok had begun to feel that whatever was happening between his mother and me was his fault. It wasn't said aloud; it was pointed out as a possibility by Sonal's psychiatrist. I was shaken out of my stupor because I hadn't even thought in that direction. Years back, when Sonal was pregnant, I was chatting with a colleague in office and the topic was about what kind of a father I thought I'd be. My answer was, *'If I am as good a father to my child as I am a husband to my wife, I will be happy.'*

She looked pleased and said that it was a great answer. But now? So much for being a good father, I thought. Or a good husband, for that matter. So, I sat Shlok down and discussed the possibility with him. I asked him point-blank if he felt responsible for any of what was happening. While he wasn't overtly feeling responsible, he was beginning to have a dog-whistled feel that some of the things were indeed his fault. Because there had been times when Sonal would be yelling at him for some reason or the other, which I wouldn't find justified. So, I would take up for Shlok whenever Sonal didn't let him be. This led him to believe that because Sonal and I were arguing over something that he had (or had not) done, the total mess was his fault.

I mentally face-palmed for not having realized something so simple. I hugged him close and told him in no uncertain terms that none of whatever had happened or was happening was his fault. That there were times when mamma and papa disagreed on certain things because mamma was unwell. That often, mamma lost her temper or got agitated or stressed for the same reason. That whatever happens in the family, it would not be his fault. That mamma and papa would try to fight lesser, but he should stop holding himself responsible for any of it.

I would have made at least twenty such statements multiple times to hammer it into him and stop him from fanning his guilt further. I made sure that he got that out of his head. I cursed myself for not giving him reason to be happy and feel secure in his life. It is a sin to have a child that small feel guilty about something that is not his fault and not recognize that. Thank God for Sonal's psychiatrist, who alerted me to the possibility for me to be able to nip this in the bud. I also kept making veiled inquiries with him more frequently after that incident, lest the feeling resurface. Thankfully, it hadn't. It still hasn't.

CHAPTER XIII

Demands On My Time

"'Nothing lasts really. Neither happiness nor despair. Not even life lasts very long. There'll come a time in the future when I shan't mind about this anymore, when I can look back and say quite peacefully and cheerfully how silly I was.' - Celia Johnson, Brief Encounter"

As for me, along with the usual compromises, there were also many demands on my time. So, if there was office work to be done, I couldn't get it home. Sonal would want me to either work from home on some days, or if I was in the office, she would have Shlok call me up to come back home early on some other days. Sonal would be scared of braving the day by herself. Her simple reasoning was that Shlok would get neglected if she lost control. Shlok wasn't old enough to take care of himself and of Sonal. So, I would be forced to agree. I would have to work from home quite often. Since my office was close by, and since I was one of the co-founders of the company, with an army of foot soldiers to support me, it was an abused privilege. I began to spend more time working from home – sometimes as many as three days a week (in a working week of five days).

Cut to the Annual Day in office. We were celebrating our 2nd Anniversary in Delhi. The celebration was in a pub, and apart from the usual food and drinks and dance, a few team members had also organized an award function – more on the lines of the Raspberries. So, there were awards for the cry baby of the office, the latecomer of the office, and so on. I won two awards that year – one which I was proud of - for being an MS-Excel maniac (for which they had an unprintable award title), and one which I wasn't proud of - for working-from-home the most number of times. There weren't any other strong contenders at all in both categories. It was all in good spirit, and people were making fun of me (and the others), and I, in turn, was mock threatening to raise their targets, but you know what? The second title didn't really sit well with me. Sure, I had my reasons, but hey! Either you have results or excuses. I didn't have results. So, my reasons amounted to nothing but excuses.

For the same reason, my work-related travel started going down too. Previously, where I was used to travelling for a week a month (sometimes to Delhi, sometimes to Bangalore and once in a while to some other country), now it was reduced to about four days every forty-five days. I was slowly losing my grip on clients outside Mumbai and had to completely depend upon my Regional Heads for effective execution in those areas. I was fortunately, blessed with very efficient Regional heads, and therefore, the business didn't suffer, but my relationships did. Since I was Head of Sales in my company, it was blasphemous. But all of that was irrelevant for me then. What was important was that Sonal (and, equally importantly, Shlok) be properly taken care of. I would have even quit my job and sat at home if required (and if I could afford it, of course). Not a very professional or ambitious thing to say, but I'm saying it anyway. That was when I should have had my head examined as well.

CHAPTER XIV

The Intensity Of The Problem – Glimpse III

"'Remember: no obstacles, only challenges.' - Steve Van Wormer, Groove"

Meanwhile, the crusade at home continued to get worse. The amount of money spent on cleaning was insanely high; we spent in one moth what other houses would spend in at least six. But just to keep peace at home, I would not question Sonal about that and let her have her way. For a long time, I was divided about whether it was the right thing to do or not. As per the books and the advice of the therapists, I ought not to have allowed that. I was encouraging it and making matters worse. But I didn't know that until then, and peace at home was more important. I am reasonably certain though that had I known what the correct course of action was I would still have been fairly lenient. I am beginning to realize that my empathy is equally a boon and a curse. I would have not wanted her to suffer too much and probably ended up making the wrong choice, as I do with Shlok sometimes.

Sonal was using copious quantities of soaps, detergents, dishwashing liquid, antiseptic solutions, face washes, shampoos, cleaning cloths, mops, garbage bags, phenol solutions, ant-repellents and various other items that were never used earlier. We were averaging about four cleaning cloths every day. All four cleaning cloths would be thrown away at the end of each day. None of them would be used even twice. Some would be used once and thrown, and others would be thrown without being used even once. Brand new cleaning cloths. Typically, the types used in other houses for a month at least.

To begin with they would be washed thoroughly with detergent – enough for a full load of clothes. They would be rinsed multiple times, and then no one apart from Sonal could touch them. If they were touched by anyone else, they would need to be rewashed. Once washed, each cleaning cloth would be used to clean only a specific room or part of the house. Once it had lived through its utility, it would be washed again with an equal amount of detergent before being discarded.

Midway through the cleaning, if she happened to get an intrusive thought, if she happened to catch an ad on TV or happened to see something sweet in a magazine, or even if the word was mentioned, a thought could get triggered, and she would feel that the cleaning cloth has something sweet on it. She would sometimes take the cleaning cloth to her tongue to verify her thought. If she had the feeling that the cloth was sweet, she would discard it and pick up another one. This could also happen to cloth that hadn't even been used at all. That would need to go too. She would end up ordering for more. Off went the discarded ones into the trashcan.

She never kept an account of how much she spent, never thought for a moment if something was amiss and never stopped herself from splurging on these things. It was a particularly disturbing thing for me to not know where the money was going. I tried to get her to keep the account of what was being spent too many times. I forced her to make a note of the expenditure for her to be able to recognize the absurdity of the extravagance. We even had fights over it. She would promise, and then forget. Or she didn't want to be bothered. Or she didn't want me to know. The exercise was undertaken many times only to stop after a point. I gave up. An uncle of mine once said that it was fortunate that I could at least afford it. True, that! Suppose I hadn't been able to? Our relationship would have crumbled long back.

Another reason for not actively and forcefully stopping her from spending was that apart from this one excess, she has never been money-minded or demanding. She has never asked for international vacations or expensive clothes or jewellery. She has always been very frugal. Happy to live in the humblest of circumstances. So, I didn't complain (much) because I realized that it was being done only because she had no control over it. It would irk me because I have always been anti-wastage. When it would get too much for me to handle, we would sometimes lock horns. To no avail. Her OCD would always win.

Just as Sonal's list of compulsions kept getting longer, so did her 'list of things to avoid'. There were many more new things that became the incubus. She would contort every issue through her weird logic to give it an OCD hue. You know the logic puzzles in which one statement seemingly doesn't have any connection to another and deduction and inference seem impossible? And then when you see the solution, you are left wondering how at all you missed the connection? That is how it was between any event in the day and OCD, as far as Sonal's mind was concerned. A friend of mine prided himself on his creative thinking and punning skills and once played a game with me. He asked me to give him any word, and he would think of an ad line for it with a pun in it. I gave him 7-8 words and he managed to think of a pun in under 10 seconds for each word. He did it beautifully. Sonal's life seemed to have become a game like that. Give me a word, and I shall connect it with my OCD and stress myself out, she seemed to say. She did it too, albeit I wouldn't call it 'beautifully'.

An immediate connection was sought and locked on between OCD and any every day event. Sonal also began to become uncomfortable with new ones of her own devising. For one, she was uncomfortable with anyone stepping into our house. Or should I say her house? I think at some level, she would have been happier if even Shlok and I were to not enter the house at all because having a clean house was her biggest priority and also the biggest reward for her, and she couldn't let anyone interfere with that. Not even us. It was a pity (for her) that we had to stay there, with her. So, we were tolerated with the greatest amount of reluctance – and just about too. But the others certainly weren't.

The first category of people to bear the brunt (and possibly the worst affected lot) was all types of servicemen like grocery delivery boys and fruit and vegetable vendors (who would carry a basket of their wares from house to house to make a sale), plumbers and electricians. They were treated with utmost contempt. Sonal would look at them with unabashed disdain. She would think that their shoes were dirty, their clothes grubby, and they were spewing filth all over. She would fret about their having come to our house after having visited others, and who knows what they had picked up on their shoes, bags and bodies from there. They could have had ants in their shoes or bags, or something else in their bags that would attract ants. Who knows when they had last washed their clothes? Their bags? Their shoes? Who knows when they had last had a bath? She had little regard for their time or for their importance in our lives. And precious little respect for them as humans, if at all.

When stars were against me sometimes, and some such service was required, she would start behaving as if the malfunction was my doing and it was my fault that those people had to be called over. She would also behave as if those men worked at my beck and call. I would get grief about when to call them and when not to call them. *'Don't call them in the morning – I feel stressed.' 'Don't call them in the afternoon – it is lunchtime.' 'Don't call them in the evening – the maid servant would have left by then.'* I would not know what to say or do. *'When do I call them then, woman?'*

Just to clarify, in India as in many other countries almost every house has a maid servant. India being a labor rich country, having a maid is so affordable that it is no longer a luxury, but almost a necessity. We had one too. So, the servicemen could be called home only at specific times. The window available to them was a small one, which was sometime in the afternoon before lunch, before the maid servant finished her work and after Sonal's morning rituals were over. They couldn't just sashay into our houses as and when they pleased. It was Sonal's house and she made sure they knew that. She made sure she got things done exactly as she wanted. When she wanted. If the servicemen didn't come on time, which was often the case since they would have had other houses to attend to, she would make it my fault, and I would be held responsible for that too.

Besides, they had to be always called only when I was at home. That was only on weekends or holidays. She would never call them herself and get the work done. She needed me to be there to handle these tasks, even though there wasn't much that I could do. She would have me call them up. Strangely, I would feel apologetic about their responses. I was damned if they declared that they couldn't come at the time Sonal wanted them to, and I was damned if they agreed to come. Tentatively, hesitantly, I would inform Sonal about their responses and brace myself for a tirade. I could never get used to being blamed for things that were not my fault (as I saw them), and I would flare up if she as much as tried to pin it on me.

Many a time, these tasks were inordinately delayed at home because either we would not call them at all (not today – tomorrow, or not tomorrow – next week) or when we did, they would be turned away at the door because they would have either come too early or too late and would have missed the window, which the poor sots would not have been aware of, to begin with. Or they would not measure up to her standards of cleanliness. Belatedly she realized that they never did, and so she had a semi-relaxed standard for these people, albeit not without grudges.

Then, when they were to come, if they had agreed to, it would be as if all hell hath broken loose. She would anxiously await their arrival by the door, peep through the eye hole nervously, pace up and down, mutter to herself about how the house would get dirty and how she would have to clean it up and no sooner would they come than she would open the door, sometimes without even waiting for them to ring the doorbell and start firing instructions, *'Leave your shoes far away from the door. Wipe your feet on the mat. Is your bag clean? Why isn't your bag washed? Are there any ants in it?'*

And so on. She would have them open their bags at the door and check them to make sure that they passed muster, and only then would she let them in. Then she would be hovering around them with a perpetual frown of despair on her face and a steady string of the *'pchht'* sound that one makes when one is unhappy, coming out of her mouth. It would irritate me sometimes, and I would say, *'What is it, Sonal? Why can't you let them do their work in peace?'*

She would ignore me, growl at me, or say something nasty and I would shut up, not wanting to argue in front of the servicemen, who would be smiling apologetically.

She would lay down newspapers for them to stand on. She would scowl visibly when their grimy feet would leave dirt stains in the wet bathroom. She would rebuke them for not maintaining hygiene. Sometimes I feared she would ask them to go away and come back only when they were cleaner. Sometimes I thought she would ask them to take a bath right there before doing their work. Sometimes, I used to think it was a wonder that these people still came over to do our work for us. Had I been in their places, I would have probably refused to work in a house like that.

One of the strangest things I've noted about these servicemen is that they are truly a messy lot. If they buy a new switch or a new pipe or anything new, they pull the item out of the packaging and throw the packet on the floor, strewing debris all over the place. They don't keep it piled neatly in one corner to be picked up and disposed off after the task is done. That peeved Sonal. She would also fret about the debris if there was any drilling work or carpentry to be done. She would ask me apprehensively, *'Kachra hoga?'* (Will they make a mess?)

All of this used to seem silly and unnecessary to me, and I would be discomfited with her behavior, her downright insolence. Was I claiming that I didn't get embarrassed easily? Sometimes I would speak for the serviceman who would be awkwardly smiling at his humiliation, and at other times, I would get irritated and snap at her for being so unconscionable. But she would be oblivious to any discomfort or ire on anyone else's part, just seeking succor in her reassurances that she was doing everything possible not to let ants inside the house. I knew then and know now that she was not choosing to be difficult. Her OCD would not allow her to take it easy and she would be making lives miserable for others because her own life was made far more miserable by her OCD and she only wanted to not have to go through the anxiety. I chose not to understand and only found fault with her.

After they left, she would get down to cleaning the place up in her own obsessive way, all the while mumbling to herself, cursing the servicemen, cursing her luck, cursing God and anyone else she could think of. Sometimes, she would somehow connect it to me and start cursing me. It would baffle me, and I would ask, '*maine kya kiya?*' (What did I do?)

It would become too much for my prickly ego to handle. I would feel a groundswell of anger rising, and we would start fighting again. She would make random arguments to support her claim, and I would argue ostensibly logically. But, in reality, my logic was nothing but a verbal rapier to hurt her feelings as she had hurt my ego. One fall out of that is that even to this date, whatever she does if it sounds remotely accusatory I begin to feel she is blaming me. We often argue just because I think she is accusing me, and she avers that she isn't. I realize now that so many instances ended with variations of '*it would become too much for my ego to handle, and we would start fighting*', when it clearly was not her fault. She had no control over her feelings since they were controlled by her OCD. What an unreasonable man, I must have seemed to her then. What an unreasonable man I seem to myself now.

Sonal also needed to check clothes that came back after ironing to ensure no ants in them. The clothes were not given to a laundry but to a small ironing shop that had a pickup and delivery service. The exact same treatment used to be meted out to him as to the other vendors. Instructions shot, insults hurled, ego atomized to smithereens. The added angst was that the humiliation would be more frequent – every two days or so. She would be particular that the bundle of clothes given for ironing was at no point in its journey kept on the floor anywhere.

Since the man serviced the entire apartment building, he would have a lot of bundles of clothes, which he would need to keep somewhere. He would keep them on the floor in the lobby of the building and then deliver them turn by turn. If Sonal ever happened to see that her bundle was placed on the floor, she would raise hell. After the clothes came back from ironing, she opened each garment and subjected it to a microscopic scrutiny for ants. Most times, there would be none, but sometimes, on a rare occasion, she would find an ant somewhere, and the whole cycle of panic attacks would start again. '*Why do you have to check?*' I would ask. She wouldn't have an answer.

She had changed her grocer because she didn't think that the first one maintained sufficient hygiene. To this date, I haven't been able to understand the difference between the two since both of them are right next to each other, and both look equally clean to me. But I am sure that in her heightened state of awareness, in her magnified worldview because of OCD, she saw a difference and hence chose the second grocer over the first.

The maid servant had a specific time when she would be let in. She was accorded no grace either and would not be let in if she came early. Even if it was just by fifteen minutes. She would have to sit outside the house and wait for those fifteen minutes before she could finally enter the house. I am pretty sure that the maid servant must have been wondering what Sonal did in those fifteen minutes. She eventually recognized the pattern. The maid was also not allowed to come late. If she was going to be late, Sonal needed to be informed well in advance to prepare herself for it. She didn't like surprises, and a change in the maid servant's schedule was too much of one for her to be comfortable with it.OCD sufferers do not like a change in pattern and Sonal was no different.

Sonal was also not comfortable with our parents and siblings coming over. So, while she would try her hardest to be nice to them (her original self making a desperate attempt to peek out of her OCD-soaked avatar), it would show in her behavior. She would not be at her social best. Lacklustre and reluctant. Plus, the invite to guests was never renewed. I am not a party-goer either, but I am reasonably outgoing. Shlok would definitely have a good time if people came over. But because of OCD, all of that had to stop.

I suppose our demeanor made it fairly clear to our relatives that they were not exactly welcome to our house. Not that we entertained too much before Sonal's OCD, but after that, all of it stopped. My parents anyway do not visit us too often. We visit them instead. But whatever little they did visit us stopped altogether. My brother and his family stopped coming over, even as infrequently as they used to too. Even my niece, who used to come over once in a while to play with Shlok stopped coming. Once again, it was us who went to visit them more.

After some time, my sister-in-law (my brother's wife), who used to be good friends with Sonal before her OCD and used to talk to her at least once a day on the phone, reduced her interactions and finally stopped calling. Or Sonal did. I cannot put a finger to who withdrew first, but relations slackened. Some years later, my brother mentioned that my sister-in-law used to feel apprehensive about calling Sonal for fear of doing something that would upset Sonal and hence had stopped calling altogether. Fair! But as a result of this, we began to feel isolated.

Sonal's parents would visit once in a while, but Sonal would be blunt with them. She felt that they did not clearly understand her problem. Because even her father was dismissive of her condition. He would shake his head in disapproval over certain things that Sonal did or did not do. So, she was not happy about them coming over either. Whatever gifts my father-in-law would get for us (fruits, biscuits, etc) would be turned down by Sonal, and they would have to take them back. No matter how many times he had to take the gifts back, he just wouldn't stop. Every time they visited, he would get something, not realizing that it was causing his daughter unspeakable stress.

'*How can we come empty-handed?*' he would ask. So, Sonal told him off once. Rudely too, I should add. She even told them not to visit her at all because entertaining guests was causing her stress, and indecorously sent them packing. So, they stopped coming too. After that day, as in the case of other relatives, we would go and visit them whenever we wanted to. Rude and reclusive. That is what we were becoming.

Daraarein daraarein hain maathe pe maula,
Marammat muqaddar ki kar do, maula!

Loosely translated - the fate lines on my forehead are riven with cracks, oh Lord! Please restore my destiny, oh Lord!

CHAPTER XV

The Intensity Of The Problem – Glimpse IV

"'All things in life are temporary. If they are going well, enjoy them, they will not last forever. If they are going wrong, don't worry, they can't last long either.'"

With each passing day, Sonal had increased obsessions and compulsions and newer things to make life more miserable for herself. Cleaning the windows would take her the longest and was the most stressful. Since the process would generate obsessive thoughts, she would end up doing them over and over again and waste even more time. She would need to wipe the entire grille everyday and apply a few lines of *Lakshman Rekha*, an anti-insect chalk. She would need to wipe all horizontal and most vertical surfaces (sometimes even walls) at home, first with wet cloth and then with dry cloth. She would need to clean the insides of the cupboards everyday too. The number of times that I have had to dissuade her from wiping wooden furniture with a wet cloth, lest the plywood furniture start rotting and bloating, is too high to even count.

The bathroom and the toilet were to be washed every day. The mopping was to be done with water that had detergent, an antiseptic and a floor cleaner in it. In large quantities. I used to think I could eat off the floor if required and would not fall sick. That is how clean our house needed to be. Every. Single. Day!

It would take her no less than two hours to clean the kitchen every night. We would finish eating by ten-thirty, and she would finish her work only by half-past midnight. One day when she was unwell, I told her that I would clean the kitchen for her. She was reluctant to entrust me with such important a responsibility, but she felt too weak to do it herself. So, she gave in to my exhortations and grudgingly agreed.

She couldn't believe me when I told her fifteen minutes later that the kitchen was done. She interrogated me on every aspect she could think of, not unlike how Sheldon from The Big Bang Theory questions Leonard about the food he is eating.

'Did you clean the platform?'

'Yes'

'Did you wipe the gas stove?'

'Yes'

'Did you arrange the vessels in the sink?'

'Yes'

'Did you wipe all the containers before keeping them on the shelf?'

'Yes'

'Did you clean the floor?'

'Yes'

But she could not believe it and was not satisfied with my answers. She had to get up and physically drag herself to the kitchen to inspect everything and make sure it was the way I had said. If it was the way she wanted it to be. I was holding my breath, feeling that any moment she would pounce upon me for something that had remained undone. Or worse, that she would find something not done well and would insist on doing it herself. She couldn't find any flaws, but she wasn't convinced that it could be done in fifteen minutes. However, I managed to convince her that even if it was not the way she wanted, it would hold for a day until she got better and did it the way she wanted to. She bought into that line of reasoning and let it go. Then, she rested. I exhaled.

The bed sheet had to be changed and every day, where earlier it used to be done once a week. She would complain that the house was dusty and the curtains were getting dirty. Hence they needed to be washed once every fortnight, if not sooner.

She would bathe four times a day. She would get up in the morning and would feel dirty. So, she would take a bath. She would bathe after lunch, after she finished cleaning in the evening, and once at night, after all her compulsions for the day were over.

She would wash her hands at least a hundred times a day. A typical hand wash bottle would last us about a day and a half, on the outside. I must admit that I have been severely ignorant about some of these things until they hit me in the face. I even realized this hand wash fetish quite late in the day. When I was leaving for office once, there was no hand wash, and I asked Sonal for it. She brought out a new bottle and kept it at the washbasin. When I returned from the office that evening, the bottle was three-fourths gone. Sometimes, I feel that had my involvement been more than superficial, we could have foreseen a lot of misery and avoided it.

Sonal had also started using up face wash excessively. She didn't feel that the hand wash was good enough to clean her hands. So, she would use face wash to clean her hands. She would also wash her face multiple times a day.

She would wash Shlok's school bag and school shoes every day. When he returned from school, the bag and the shoes would be checked thoroughly for any signs of ants / dirt / sweets. These two items in particular, would go straight into the bathroom for their daily wash. Sometimes, because of that, Shlok would not have a dry pair of shoes to wear the following day. He would end up needing to wear the same wet pair (which he wouldn't like at all and would complain only to be shouted at by Sonal) or non-school shoes (which he was scared of being rebuked for by the teachers, should any of them happen to spot it). No amount of reasoning with her in this ever helped. She always quietly listened to everything I had to say but then continued to do what she wanted.

One simple solution to this problem was to get an additional set of each item. But that would have amounted to fanning the fire. That would be a validation of her need to wash them every day, an endorsement of her irrational behavior, if you may, and that would have been the wrong thing to do. So, I did not even suggest the option. In retrospect though, maybe I should have. It would have encouraged and enabled her OCD, yes, but at least my son would have had dry shoes to wear to school every day. It is not as if this was the only compulsion she was doing. It is not as if allowing her this would have led to her OCD getting significantly worse. Poor judgment on my part; that is all this was. He was too young to remember and hold it against us, but I hold every poor bit of parenting against myself. Not to be self-critical, but just to remind myself of the fact that I was not as perfect as I used to think I was.

On one occasion, out of stubbornness, I forbade Sonal from washing Shlok's school bag because I thought it was foolish that the bag should be washed every day. Not required, wasteful and crazy. Sonal argued about the need to. One word led to another, and soon we were having a shouting match. I do not know what possessed Sonal, but because I wouldn't let her have her way, things got so out of hand, and Sonal got so agitated that she picked up the same bag and whacked me on the back with it. She defiantly asked me, '*You won't let me wash this bag, is it? Let me see how you will stop me.*'

I was sitting on the floor polishing my shoes and hence a sitting duck for her ire. Such was the control of OCD over her that Sonal, who was hitherto a meek, submissive person, who was always respectful of me, was forced to hit me under the command of her OCD. OCD had her in its clutches nice and proper and, like any addiction, overrode all her other sensibilities. I do not know where the control came from, but I kept quiet and did not retaliate. I don't know where my ego went into hiding. I was close to getting up and slapping her. But suddenly, I felt deflated and didn't see the point in that. I think it was only because Shlok was around that I managed that supreme degree of self-control.

We were eating out more and more often. She would just not have the strength to cook after a long day. It wasn't so much the cooking that would sap her but the cleaning before and after. After having spent the entire day mired in her enervating compulsions, the last thing she wanted was to create more work by cooking. So, a few restaurants became our daily haunts. Far from being a celebration, which is what eating out ideally should be, it used to be a way of letting Sonal have some respite from the stress that she used to feel just trying to survive the day. Regardless of whether we enjoyed it or not, we would go.

We could also have ordered for food to be delivered home. But that was unacceptable to Sonal too because if we ate at home, she would need to go through her kitchen cleaning routine anyway. So, It always had to be eating outside. Even when I was tired or sometimes even unwell and, therefore, unwilling to go out. No dice! Can't cook, won't cook. We go out or we don't eat. No discussions entertained.

On Saturdays and Sundays, when I was at home, I would see just how much she was getting sucked into the vortex of her compulsions. We would eat lunch at around 3.30 PM (since that was the time when she would finish the first leg of her work). Most times, we had to make do with the leftovers of the previous night. Or there were quick fixes like *parathas* with curd or Maggi instant noodles. The best solution to this problem (from Sonal's point of view, not mine) was to go out somewhere in the morning itself.

Mornings were the most difficult for her. She felt as if someone was physically pushing her and she could not resist the push unless she ran away from the situation. To some mall for some window shopping. Or to watch a movie. Or any other place. It didn't matter where. It didn't matter what we did. It didn't matter even if we did nothing. Even if it meant wasting our time away, it was alright with her. As long as she didn't have to be at home (ours or someone else's – What's the point of going from one house to another, she would quip) and face the house and the tasks before her.

She chose to avoid rather than face. We would return only late at night after dinner so that she would not have to cook and so that she would be too tired to bother about cleaning.

We also tried to keep a cook for a few days because I used to get upset for having to eat out so often. On weekdays, I wasn't eating home food for lunch when in the office anyway and would have preferred '*ghar ka khaana*' at least for dinner and on weekends. Plus, I repeat, I wasn't in favor of Shlok eating unhealthy food all the time. So, I insisted that we would hire a cook if Sonal wasn't cooking. We hired a middle-aged cook who was also cooking for one of our neighbors. But the blunderbuss that he was, he would leave a huge mess in the kitchen, and Sonal would get stressed, what with having to clean up. There would be vegetable trash and wheat flour strewn all over the kitchen platform. Even a fairly clean platform used to take a lot of time for Sonal to clean. An actually untidy platform took hours. Far more time than the time saved by the cook. The stress caused was also higher than the stress-relief on account of ready food being available. So, like with so many others who could not help us, the cook was dumped as well.

For a few days after that, we ordered for dinner from a lady who cooked at home and home-delivered in our neck of the woods. She was suggested to us by a friend of Sonal's, and we found her food quite alright. She also used to stay quite close by, and therefore, the food used to be still hot by the time it was delivered to us. We needed to inform her only a couple of hours in advance, and she would deliver. So, it suited us fine. At least for those days we had home-cooked food. But there was precious little variety in the food that she sent. All the *dals* tasted similar. It was insipid fare most of the time. Shlok soon got bored of eating the same food every day. Not that it was her fault that the food lacked punch. She charged too little to be able to afford rich delicacies.

Shlok was not wrong about not finding the food appetizing enough. It wasn't. But the angel that he is, he would make his displeasure known but eat whatever was served. Whereas Sonal's OCD was making life difficult for us, our life's greatest blessing was Shlok - forever compliant and happy despite that. When I used to wake him up in the morning, he would open his eyes, see me, and give me a big, wide smile. He would hold out his arms for me to pick him up and for ten minutes after that he would be in my arms, hugging me, sleeping with head resting on my shoulder. Even the memory fills me up right now. Anyway, the food that we were ordering was just not cutting it after a few days. So, we had to stop getting food from her as well.

Once again, we resorted to eating out as often as Sonal pleased. Or rather, as her OCD pleased.

CHAPTER XVI

Our Not-So-Accommodating Neighborhood

"'A bad neighbor is a misfortune, as much as a good one is a great blessing.' - Hesiod"

As bad luck would have it, we also had neighbors who were less hygiene-conscious than even average people would be. That made matters worse for Sonal. Sometimes we would find open pizza boxes with leftovers in them placed on the staircase. At other times, the neighbor's kid above would eat a chocolate and throw the chocolate wrapper out of the window, and it would land on our window sill. All of this would be difficult for Sonal to tolerate. There was a time when I was at work and received a call from home with a scared and crying Shlok on the other side, begging me to come home because mamma was stressed. I could hear Sonal crying and yelling curses in the background because some such act of indiscretion had been committed by the neighbors resulting in a panic attack and hysterics. I left the office immediately and made my way home. Worrying all the way about both Sonal and Shlok, and wondering if the bad *karmas* of our past lives were catching up with us. As soon as I reached home, both of them wailed and came to hug me. I held both of them close to me to calm them down telling them that it was okay and there was no need to worry. Despite our fights and distancing, I could feel the need in her hugs when she was panicking and I also felt protective of her.

All the changes in Sonal could be featured in 'before-and-after' ads. Before Sonal was unwell, our next-door neighbor had once entrusted Sonal with the responsibility of watering her plant while she was away on vacation. We had brought the plant to our house to make it easier to do so. Sonal made sure that she took good care of the plant. When Sonal takes up responsibility, she ensures that she does justice to it. Or else, she doesn't take up the responsibility at all. There's no midway. No half-hearted efforts. So, she tended to the plant well.

The first time that is. When the same neighbor was going for a vacation again, this time after Sonal became ill, Sonal wasn't sure if she could handle the responsibility. She told the neighbor so. She had reservations because she thought the soil, the plant, or both would attract ants, so she was hesitant. The neighbor was aware of Sonal's problem at a peripheral level, so she did not insist. She, however, left the keys to her house with Sonal and asked if Sonal would water the plant in her home. That was acceptable to Sonal. Sonal didn't mind going over to her house to water the plant once a day. But one look at the plant on the first day made Sonal cringe in fear because there were hundreds of ants in the soil and in the sink, where the plant was kept. Sonal all but fainted, and the responsibility was immediately transferred to me. I had to water the plant every evening after I returned from work.

Not surprisingly, every time I started to open the neighbor's door, I would be issued strict instructions about how far to stand, what to touch, what not to touch, wipe my feet before entering home and so on. Every day, she would also grumble about how her neighbor didn't maintain hygiene. Thank God, I didn't keep the plant in my house, she would say. It didn't take Sonal too long to write people off her list. Or too much. One small mistake, and you could be ticked off of her list of favorite (or even bearable) people. But since this neighbor was a dear friend, she wasn't written off. However, a distance did creep in.

While one could even think of controlling the neighbors' activities, how could one control the activities of birds? Sometimes, a crow would come and drop a piece of *chapati* on the window. At other times, it would be a piece of meat or some bone. Sometimes, pigeons would come by the window, and their droppings would dirty the place. Sonal would go berserk. These things started affecting her so much that she began to wash windows everyday with bucketsful of water. The residents below started complaining that their clothes that had been put out for drying were getting wet and dirty with the water that Sonal was using, but she didn't care. She would pick up fights with people, curse them for complaining, expect me to be by her side and fight back with those neighbors (who were probably correct in the first place) but not give up her compulsion.

Again the dilemma - should I have supported my wife (thereby enabling her OCD) or opposed her? I opposed her. Not because it was good for her but because I was beginning to consider myself on the opposite side of her. It was soon becoming Sonal versus the rest of the world (including me who was supposed to be on her side).

There was a time in the distant past (oh god - how far away in the past that seems now) when she would reject cabs if they did not have a music system to play music. Now if she were going out, she would reject a great many cabs if she thought that they weren't clean enough. She would give a once over to the cabs from outside and inside. If there was anything that met her disapproval in any part of the cab, whether she came directly in touch with her or not, she would reject it. There have been times when we would have rejected five or six cabs before she finally got into one that met her standards of hygiene. For the ones she rejected, she would harangue the drivers too about how unclean their cabs were.

Soon, the problem became so severe that sometimes, she would throw away handbags that she carried or the shoes she wore if the obsession consumed her. If she were walking on the road and she happened to see either an open garbage bin or a mango seller or a cake shop or a child eating chocolates or one of many such small things, she would feel that her handbag or her shoes were contaminated. She would see images of sugar syrup, trash or mango juice contaminating her belongings and she would be too stressed to continue to use them. She could not shrug off that feeling and would ultimately find peace only when she discarded the item. So, she would end up throwing away all expensive handbags, purses and shoes.

I would see her wearing new sandals with alarming regularity. When I would ask her about it, she would initially tell me that the sandals broke and were with the cobbler. Upon pressing later she would admit that she had discarded them. It would take her a lot of courage to admit it because I would almost always get pissed off. But I now realize that it was like a sleepwalker's trance for her. She would get so dazed with stress that she wouldn't understand what was to be done, and throwing her sandals away was the only thing she could think of doing.

She had become argumentative and churlish.

With anyone who opposed anything that she did. Like neighbors who complained about her washing windows.

With people who caused her stress. Like neighbors who threw chocolate wrappers or left pizza boxes outside.

With people who she thought could cause her stress. Like plumbers, electricians, vegetable vendors, auto drivers, etc.

With anyone whom she could bully. Like Shlok. Her parents. And me.

It is only a sense of duty towards my wife that pushed me to plod on and look for a way to put together the ragged life that we were leading and salvage the *joie de vivre* that was being filched out of our lives, one dollop at a time. Often (often is two or three times daily), my machismo would step out rebelling against the slavish treatment, and fights would ensue that would go nowhere and not help at all. They would just result in souring an already soured relationship.

Then we were told about yet another psychiatrist (DM) who changed our life. Not directly, but he did.

CHAPTER XVII

Enter Doctor DM

"'The most fantastic, magical things can happen, and it all starts with a wish.' - Jiminy Cricket from Pinocchio"

We were desperate now to find someone who would help us out of the quicksand that we seemed to be getting deeper and deeper into. During one such discussion with a friend, he referred me to DM, who he said had provided a lot of relief to his wife, albeit for a different problem. His wife has been suffering from a severe back problem, and because of that, she had gone into depression. Apparently DM had helped her out of it. Since I was clutching at straws, I jumped at the prospect of getting a fresh perspective, and we said to ourselves – who knows?

That is how I found myself in the office of this bespectacled, salt-and-pepper haired, diminutive and soft-spoken but assertive and no-nonsense DM who seemed to know what he was talking about. I had my first meeting with him all by myself. The clinic was in a residential complex, and one of the rooms was his cabin. It was a nice, dimly lit and comfortably air-conditioned room. There was a couch there too. A fish tank too. The atmosphere was friendly and snug. For the first time, I felt I was in the room of an actual psychiatrist.

I went to him alone at first so as to save Sonal some stress of having to relate her entire story to yet another person. If I didn't find him worthy of continuing with, Sonal would not need to go there at all. I didn't want to put Sonal through unnecessary struggle if I could help it. He heard me out patiently and then suggested that I return with Sonal. Some of the things he said made a lot of sense, and he seemed capable. Having seen so many doctors in the not distant past, I had developed some kind of understanding about how these doctors were to be evaluated, and in my proprietary and undocumented system of evaluation, DM scored well. Or am I kidding myself? I had so many false starts. Anyway, I decided to give him a go, given that I was starved for choices anyway.

So, Sonal met him too. She also concurred with my evaluation of him and agreed to keep visiting him for treatment. She went to him for sessions where she would talk to him, and he would counsel her and also prescribe medication. His ideas and counseling style were also different. He would tell Sonal how important an ant is in the ecosystem or that we should consider keeping an ant farm as a hobby. From him, we learnt about three important things that had strangely not been mentioned by anyone else before - CBT, ERP, Brain Lock (a book on the 4 step method to work on OCD).

DM educated us about Cognitive Behavioral Therapy and Exposure and Response Prevention but stated honestly enough that he wasn't trained in administering it and no one else in Mumbai was either. According to him, therefore, we had two choices. We could continue treatment with him and also keep working on our self using Brain Lock. Or, we could go to the only institute in the country known to conduct ERP effectively – NIMHANS (National Institute of Mental Health and Neurological Sciences), the nerve centre of mental health in India, in Bangalore.

He informed us that the OCD department at NIMHANS was headed by a doctor, Dr. Y.S.R. Janardhan Reddy, who is one of the best in the world. Subsequently, some research on the internet also revealed a number of books on OCD authored by Dr. Reddy, which was impressive.

DM also told us that there was a six to eight-week schedule of therapy where therapists systematically administered therapy to the sufferer. One could either stay in living quarters within the hospital premises or rent a house outside and go in for outpatient therapy, or one could get admitted to the hospital through which extensive therapy was possible, through a group of counselors specializing in the subject.

Although he did say that no one in Mumbai was capable enough to conduct ERP, I did some basic research on the internet and looked up a few names. DM pooh-poohed the names that I rattled off. Not satisfied, I spoke to a couple of counselors that we had spoken to in the past. DM seemed to be right. There didn't seem to be anyone in Mumbai who was an ERP specialist. We found CBT specialists (including EE) but not ERP specialists.

Since we were also continuing thus far with GG, I wanted to check what he had in mind too. I spoke to him once and asked him what the way forward with Sonal would be, given that there was no apparent progress. He mentioned that he would need to start some therapy with her. Good. That was encouraging. I asked him which therapy he would start with Sonal.

I was hoping against hope that he would say ERP. That my dreams would be answered. That I would find our *nirvana* right here, in Mumbai. Therefore, my bubble of hope burst when he neither mentioned CBT nor

ERP. Nor did he name any other therapy. Either I was tired of his shenanigans and wanted to steer clear of his wishy-washy rhetoric, or he did sound evasive and hackneyed, which buttressed my decision to move on. That point was the turning point for me and whatever little faith I reposed in him until that point vanished. The wheels had come off. So, he was ticked off our list too.

CHAPTER XVIII

Exploring The Bangalore Option

"'Not all those who wander are lost.'– J.R.R. Tolkien"

Out of the two options suggested by DM, we continued with the first one for a bit. That was - a combination of treatment with him and self-treatment through Brain Lock. But all the while, a thought nagged at my brain that Bangalore is not so far from Mumbai. It is in India, after all. Plus, I had good friends in Bangalore whom I could depend upon for help, if required. I didn't want to reach a stage where I was cursing myself not to have tried something that was so close by and so easily doable. Even if this were as far as the US we were talking about, it may have made sense to go there given Sonal's condition. Hence, not to try Bangalore seemed short-sighted and foolish.

Eight weeks wasn't too long a time frame either. Even if she didn't recover fully (and frankly, seeing her condition, I was more than sure that she wouldn't come out of it in eight weeks just like that) and she was able to see just 40-60% improvement, at least we would know how it is done, and we could continue the balance treatment in Mumbai. I discussed it with a couple of friends, including the ones in Bangalore. They also agreed with me. Everyone had the same opinion. How does it hurt to try? So, I reached a decision. To give Bangalore a go. In for a penny, in for a pound.

Sure, there were practical considerations like my job, Shlok's school, the transfer, finances, etc. But Sonal's treatment was top priority, and everything else seemed secondary. Maybe it would work, maybe it would not. What did we have to lose? We decided to make an exploratory trip to Bangalore. I applied for leave in office, which was easy. On the D-day, the three of us (Sonal, Shlok and I) headed to Bangalore - to meet the famous Dr. Reddy and also to conduct a recce to assess living conditions. I felt quite comfortable about settling in Bangalore, but Sonal needed to be comfortable. So, this trip was also to acclimatize her to the garden city of India.

We stayed over at my friend's house. He very considerately came to pick us up from the airport and took us to his house. We had the use of his car too, which was a blessing. On the following day, he drove us to NIMHANS. Not having to worry about the nitty-gritty like this made the process far smoother than I could have imagined.

The experience at NIMHANS was every bit the type you would expect from a Government-run institution in India. Hordes of people queuing up for registration and waiting for their preliminary consultation. Literally hordes. There was no place to sit or even stand properly and there was poor crowd management by whatever paltry security was available. We had to run around to figure out where to go. We went to three different places, and Sonal was examined by three separate people before her file was made. My apprehension simply was that such an environment might be a put-off for Sonal, she might change her mind, and the process would have ended even before it had begun. But I guess I did her an injustice there because her resolve continued to be strong, and she braved the rigor. Her steel was attempting to re-emerge. A good sign.

Finally, we figured out where we were supposed to go. After waiting there for a while, hoping that we would be called soon (which didn't seem possible, seeing the milieu), I asked around and found out that if there is a recommendation letter from the previous psychiatrist not only do you get sent in faster but meeting the doctor you want to meet is also easier. Or else, in the preliminary consultation, the junior doctor might just refer you to any doctor he deems fit. That would have defeated the purpose, and I saw an urgent need to speak to DM from Mumbai for a letter of reference for Dr. Reddy.

I immediately called him up, gave him the background, and requested a letter. I was a little unsure of his co-operation since we had kept it from him that we would be making a visit to Bangalore. To my surprise, however, he readily obliged, and promptly sent me an email. Within the next fifteen minutes, I was armed with a reference letter from DM on my phone, addressed to Dr. Reddy. There are many people who deserve a truckload of thanks for having helped Sonal. DM's name moved a few notches up because of this.

Thus armed with the reference letter on my Blackberry phone, we headed for the preliminary consultation in a small dingy room (as hospitals are wont to be) that smacked every inch of what it was – a *sarkari* hospital. The junior doctor, and pardon me for being so judgmental based on appearances alone, did not look like someone with whom I would want to trust Sonal's mental health. However, I was pleasantly surprised to find him knowledgeable and intelligent enough to make a quick and accurate assessment of Sonal's problem (and I mentally kicked myself for mistrusting his abilities earlier – that'll teach me not to be judgmental about appearances). When I also showed him the letter of reference from DM, we were promptly whisked away to an area outside the offices of the illustrious Dr. Reddy.

This place was much cleaner and seemed more in line with what Sonal would be comfortable with. I was relieved that she would have to come here for treatment and not where we had just come from. There was a waiting room where we were made to wait for a while. Soon enough, we were escorted into a chamber where there were two young doctors. They were assisting Dr. Reddy, we got to know and they would be doing the preliminary assessment.

The first one was still finishing his studies. He had an American accent, and he spoke to us about things other than OCD. I suppose he wanted us to feel comfortable. He was a kind boy. Seemed barely out of his teens. He asked us questions such as how we would manage Shlok's schooling and my job if we moved. He also spoke a bit to Shlok, though he clearly seemed uncomfortable. His earnestness and attempt to make us feel comfortable combined with his awkwardness made me smile. He advised us on what we could do to manage the move. Nothing that we hadn't already thought through, but it was kind of him to make the suggestions anyway. That was a reassuring sign for Sonal that the doctors seemed to be caring.

The second doctor had a smiling disposition, too, and he too was gaining experience under Dr Reddy. He mentioned that everyone in their department was aware of Sonal's case. I figured that it was probably because of the email we had sent to Dr. Reddy. Again, reassuring to know that it would be a string of doctors with varied experiences, which would be looking at Sonal's case. Again, a positive feeling.

Both these doctors again made notes on the case history, asking about all doctors and all medicines prescribed until then. We carried all papers of Sonal's treatment thus far and gave them all the details. Also, the Y-BOCS (Yale-Brown Obsessive Compulsive Scale) test was conducted, which helps determine the presence and severity of the OCD symptoms. The test has ten questions, which need to be rated from 0 (no symptoms) to 4 (extreme symptoms). Depending upon how high the score is, the results are interpreted, and treatment is suggested. From what I could see, Sonal rated pretty high up. Her score on her first test was 28 out of 40, indicative of severe OCD. It was way too high, and I was glad we were doing the right thing by seeking help from the best doctor in the country.

After a long, long wait, we were summoned to Dr. Reddy's cabin. We were finally face-to-face with the man. Dr. Reddy was brisk in his approach. Once again, I was afraid that Sonal would not take kindly to his demeanor and might want to drop the idea of being treated there altogether, and I did sense dissent. When Dr. Reddy was explaining ERP to us, Sonal seemed a little uncomfortable, and Dr. Reddy asked her why. She said she would be willing to do the therapy if she is not *forced* to go into a forest. Her emphasis was on the word forced. She was clear about that right from the beginning. That she should not be forced to do anything. If she was forced, she would run away was her standard threat. To this statement of not being forced to go into a forest, Dr. Reddy (who thought the emphasis was on 'go into a forest') said, '*We might not force you to go into a forest, but we might force you to eat a gulaab jaamun.*'

Buzzz! *Galat jawaab*. For Sonal, first of all, it seemed like there would be some loss of independence as the doctors might insist on certain specific actions which she would have to perform, even if unwillingly. Secondly, by now, the mere mention of these sweets was disquieting for Sonal, and the doctor touched a raw nerve. Stepping out of the office of Dr. Reddy, I saw that Sonal was firming up her resolve not to come to NIMHANS. She voiced her usual contention, '*I will not allow anyone to force me into anything, and if anyone tries it, I will run away.*' I told her in as soothing a voice as I could, '*No one will force you to do anything against your wishes. Things will proceed at your pace.*' This didn't seem to convince her, and it left me a little worried but still strongly determined to get her treated at NIMHANS. But, Sonal grudgingly agreed to undergo the treatment. With the same caveat. Or threat. If she was forced, she would stop treatment altogether and go back to Mumbai.

Dr. Reddy had changed Sonal's medication too, stating that the current medication was inadequate. He started Sonal on 50 mg of a medicine (Sertraline) and said it was the lowest dose. He mentioned that it would need to be taken up to 200 mg eventually and hence compliance on Sonal's part to take medicines on time and regularly was critical. Sonal agreed to give up the old prescription and start following the new prescription, which was an implicit commitment in itself. Thank God for small mercies. Small wins at a time. With hope in our hearts and a new spring in our steps (at least mine), we returned to Mumbai.

CHAPTER XIX

Moving To Bangalore

"Every new beginning comes from some other beginning's end.' - Seneca"

Even after returning to Mumbai, we had a few discussions on the subject. Sonal seemed forever reluctant to move bag and baggage to Bangalore. At the best of times, even small changes to routine were anxiety inducing for Sonal. This, then was a major shift. She would dilly-dally on the decision, and we would get into lengthy discussions that would sometimes turn into arguments on why Bangalore would be good for her. It was mentally exhausting to convince her over and over, but it had to be done. I can only imagine now how tiring it must have been for her. She would concede some points and then go back to square one. This happened many times, and I oscillated between relief and frustration with amazing frequency. Finally, after a zillion entreaties, she willed herself to believe that everything would be alright and agreed to move. Phew! I crossed my fingers that she should not change her mind again.

The next step - handle the ancillary issues. Issue number one was Shlok's school. I sought an appointment from Shlok's school principal and met her. After having briefly explained the situation to her, I asked her if it would be possible for Shlok to either be excused from attending school for four months since it was just four months left for his academic year to end or if that wasn't possible, get re-admission to the same school when we returned from Bangalore.

I was happy when she said that she would be happy to provide re-admission to Shlok. Worked well for me. That was one huge burden off my chest, knowing how difficult school admissions in Mumbai are. Changing schools is even more difficult, and I was apprehensive of Shlok's having to miss a year if we couldn't manage admissions on time. Thankfully, that problem would not arise now because of this kind woman. She also got her secretary to make a photocopy of all ICSE board schools in Bangalore that I could go to and check for Shlok's admission. She gave me her email ID and asked me to write to her in case I needed any help. She asked me if we had seen AA for Sonal's treatment. Like I said, AA was famous. But we knew that she wasn't good enough for Sonal. It was nevertheless, kind of the principal to suggest her name. God bless her! I thanked her profusely for her help, completed the formalities and struck Shlok's name off from the school. One major umbilical cord was cut.

It took a while to convince Shlok though. Much as he didn't want to complain, the purest drop of godliness as he is, he could not contain his sadness at having to leave his friends and move to a new school where he knew no one. He wasn't disagreeing, but he didn't want to agree. He cried for a long time and buried his head in my shoulder, and I'd be lying if I said I didn't feel my eyes moisten. As I write this, I feel my eyes moisten again. What was worse was that I couldn't even entice him into having an ice cream or chocolate to take his mind off. I hugged him tight and rocked him in my arms, whispering pacifying words for a long, long time. I was beginning to lose track of the number of times a six-year-old had to adjust for his mother. The scale was nowhere near balanced, and it was gut wrenching to make him go through it all. But Sonal's health was the most important concern, no matter how many sacrifices anyone had to make. I was fervently hoping that my child's sacrifices would be worth the trouble.

Next, I needed to tackle my job. I had informed my boss about the whole issue and we were still navigating how we would handle it all. I wasn't sure if it made sense to ask for a transfer, given that our major clients were in Mumbai and Delhi. A transfer to Delhi would have been easier, I thought but not to Bangalore. So, I told my boss that I wanted to resign. He was shocked and refused to accept my resignation. I told him that I would be away for at least four to six months, and during that time, I would not be able to contribute too much, if at all. He said he would speak to the investors – I was a co-founder after all and quitting like that wouldn't look good for the company in the industry. A day later, he told me that I didn't need to resign and that I could go to Bangalore and work from home there. That I should contribute as much as I could and he would handle the work in my absence. Mighty kind of him, I should say. God bless him for that. I made sure I provided a detailed handover to him and my team and promised to put in as much as I could. Another major issue was taken care of; a big, big load off my chest.

Since the four big tasks out of the five, that the decision to move to Bangalore largely depended upon seemed to be handled (getting Sonal's agreement, managing Shlok's school in Mumbai, getting Shlok's agreement (albeit with reluctance) and managing my job), the next step was to accomplish the last task. Secure admission for Shlok to a school in Bangalore. That job was easier said than done because it was mid-term, and the second semester had already begun. I wasn't even sure if he would get admissions anywhere, and I was also ready to have him repeat a year if required. Once again, there was no regard for how troublesome repeating a year would be for the child. We were almost blind to his needs, much as I tried to do the right things. Before that, I knew I would be trying my hardest to get him into a good school in Bangalore.

So, I made a solo trip to Bangalore. To scout for schools that would allow mid-term admission to grade II. I also needed to look for a place to stay. Since it would be a longish stay in Bangalore after we moved, we couldn't obviously pile on to my friend as we had when we had wanted to explore NIMHANS or live in a hotel, which would prove to be expensive. We had decided not to stay in the institution premises either because apart from being quite shabby and also not offering enough value for money, there were loads of ants there.

I was on the road practically all day for three days, armed with a classifieds tabloid for houses on rent and the list that Shlok's school principal from Mumbai had so kindly given me for school admissions in Bangalore. It was tiring work. I was turned away from many schools because they did not allow mid-term admissions, and some of the houses that I saw also were no good. But hard work paid off, and I managed to find a few good houses and a few seemingly good schools in the Koramangala / Sarjapur Road areas, which were close to NIMHANS. I picked up their prospectuses and forms for our next visit to Bangalore.

I was quite happy with myself and called up Sonal to share the good news. Instead, she gave me a jolt. She told me that she had decided against moving. Again. Bam! The powers-that-be seemed to be enjoying at my expense, sending across challenge after new challenge. They seemed to be waiting for things to get easier for me before they threw a new curved ball my way. I didn't know whether to be amused or frustrated at the way fate seemed to be mocking me in novel ways every day. I was discussing this with a friend and he asked me,

'So, what are you going to do?'

'I'm going to ensure that we come to Bangalore for Sonal's treatment. Whatever it takes.'

'Good. I completely agree with you and I was hoping you would say that'.

In the face of opposition and total despair from all sides, even the slightest hint of support from any corner does wonders for confidence. I felt empowered afresh when he said this. I was even more firmly resolved to get Sonal to Bangalore. Back in Mumbai, I had a long discussion with Sonal again, which seemed to be a stalemate. I kept requesting, and Sonal kept refusing. We had our tickets booked. The packers and movers had been organized. Shlok's name had been struck off from his school in Mumbai, and we had a leaving certificate in hand. I had handed over all my responsibilities to my boss at work. Goodbyes were said to friends and family. Now this *naatak*. After many sessions and many hours of cajoling, fighting, explaining and browbeating, I finally got her to agree.

Over the next two days, I organized everything. Called the packers and movers to pack our stuff to be transported to Bangalore and said goodbye to all friends and family. Bangalore, here we come! Shortly thereafter, we left for Bangalore, bag and baggage. To achieve our Holy Grail.

The Middle

CHAPTER XX

The First Few Days In Bangalore

"'What happened to us? Life! And we are dealing with it the best way we can.' - The Lying Game (2011)"

When we first landed in Bangalore in December 2010, I had booked a room for a few days in the company guest house. But I knew that we would have to move out of that place soon because there were ants in the small garden outside. Wherever we went, ants followed us. That is hardly surprising, though. Fun fact - there are approximately one million ants to every human being on earth. To add to that, we were in the garden city of India after all. So, good luck trying to avoid running into them.

I showed Sonal a few apartments and hoped we would move in soon. But that wasn't happening as I began to realize how picky Sonal was. We moved into another guest house, which was ant-free but also more expensive. I was hoping that it would be a short stay. This was one more hope that was going to be shattered, though. My hope of a short stay was another one at which God was laughing his guts out.

Living with Sonal was becoming increasingly stressful for me, too, by then. She would go to bed in a foul mood and wake up in a fouler mood. Anything I said or did was misinterpreted, and there would be hell to pay for. If I am fair to her though, anything she said was also misinterpreted by me often. There was rarely anything said by one person that the other was not reading sinister meanings into. She decided she didn't want to talk to anyone from our families. No one was allowed to call us up. No one called. When I did receive a call, I would move away from where she was and spoke in hushed tones, almost as if I was committing a crime by being on the phone. Sonal felt enslaved by her OCD, and I felt enslaved by Sonal. My selfishness was making me blind to the extent of her suffering. Sure I was there with her making sacrifices and wanting her to get well. But I did not understand the quantum of her suffering well enough. I chose to dwell on the feeling of being enslaved. I only shudder to think what Shlok was going through, caught in the crossfire, as he was then.

Sonal hated (not disliked, hated) Bangalore because it was 'squalid and putrid' (in places, it was), and there were so many trees. Did I mention that walking under trees was a problem with Sonal? Because there could be ants on trees and the ants on the trees could fall on her if she walked under those trees. Since Bangalore has so many trees she had another excuse to not want to stay there.

Then came the house hunting. Some of the houses we saw were downright dirty. Some of them had ants in them. Some of them had a lot of tree cover in the complex. Some of them had trees right outside the window. If some house was good, it was too large. A large house meant more cleaning and hence would be unacceptable. It seemed to me that there was no house that we would be able to say yes to at the rate at which Sonal was rejecting the houses. Left to myself, I would have happily taken up any of the houses I had seen. To my mind, one was more beautiful than the other. But not for Sonal. Sonal wanted a small house so that cleaning the house would be simpler. It was no small irony that small houses were available only in relatively older apartment complexes, or independent houses, which were not clean or had ants in them. The cleaner complexes all had larger apartments.

What once chilled me to the bone was her statement that she would rather live in a small one-room apartment with no windows. It still gives me goose-bumps to realize how she was treading a fine line between sanity and insanity and how serious she was about this one-room accommodation. I could only picture a spotless white, padded, windowless room and Sonal in a straitjacket sitting in a corner mumbling to herself in an asylum. As seen in movies. Or worse, in a psychiatric facility like the one we saw where GG practiced. Shudder!

It was purely our good fortune that we finally found a place she liked in a complex she liked. She liked the complex because it had a housekeeping team available round the clock that would keep the place spic and span. No trash anywhere, no tobacco, *gutka* or *paan* spit marks anywhere, no dirt anywhere. There were no trees by the window, no ants visible anywhere, just the right size. (Maybe not, but she agreed to it). It was a larger apartment than we have ever stayed in, but she didn't mind the size because it was so clean. Thank God for small mercies.

But even after we found this place, she was hesitant to move into it, and we spent four additional days in the guest house just because the new home was not set up and Sonal wanted a cup of tea first thing in the morning, which wasn't possible in the new house. Those have been the most expensive four cups of tea I have ever needed to buy (about 100 dollars a cup). The extravagance appalled me but Sonal's sheer helplessness, masked as anger, left me with no choice either.

The apartment that we finalized upon was in a housing complex that was referred to us by the dean of one of the new schools I had visited. This place was not far from the school. The school was recommended by a friend who had both kids there. Since the school was new, getting admission was not a problem, even mid-year. So, we also secured admission for Shlok in that school. It was a beautiful school with a large playground and clean classrooms. The student-to-teacher ratio was also good, and the impression that the faculty made on us was good too. Plus, there was a convenient bus service to the school. So, another hurdle was sorted.

At long last, we finally moved, and I was happy to be free of the everyday guest house expense. Since the house was cleaned to her satisfaction, I thought at least Sonal would not spend so much time cleaning it and would have adequate time for therapy. But that wasn't to be. Sonal would not only spend hours cleaning up the house but, when the opportunity presented itself, also get me to lend a helping hand for her compulsions. But the standard of hygiene maintained by the society suited Sonal, and I was thankful that at least that bit would be trouble-free for us.

Imagine my horror, therefore when one late evening, after both Sonal and Shlok had slept off, I saw long a string of big, black ants on the wall right outside the bedroom balcony. A long line of them. It may have been close to a hundred. Or more. Oh God, please, no! Please! Why is this happening to me? If Sonal were to see that, not only would something terrible happen to her health-wise, but we would probably also have to leave the house and find another house or, worse, move back to Mumbai. It was unbelievable how heavily the odds were stacked against us. What have I done to deserve this?

I had a task on my hands. I needed to get rid of the ants and plug the holes so that they would not return. I also needed to do it quietly so that Sonal did not wake up. If she did, I was doomed. So, carefully and cautiously, I got the broom and swept off the ants with it, as many as I could. I admit with some viciousness. To cause them some pain, if I could. Causing them pain wouldn't relieve us of our pain, but who cared? I needed to take my frustration and annoyance out on someone. Much to the misfortune of those ants, they had become a blight in our lives, and I was not about to let them add more troubles to our already difficult existence. So, I got rid of them with great ferocity. Having done that, I plugged whatever holes I could find with soft soap. Good!

I was just using moonlight as my source of light, and since this was outside the balcony on one side, I didn't even have a good foothold or a handhold. Precariously perched. While I was filling up the crevices, I was also conscious not to lean over too much or else it would have been goodbye world for me. Hence, I couldn't even reach as far as I would have liked to. So, I did what I could under the circumstances and hoped for the best.

After that, I took the risk of switching on the light in the balcony to see if some dead ants had fallen over there. They had. I swept the place clean with the broom and thanked my good luck for having had the foresight to check.

In the morning, I checked to see if there was still a line of ants outside the balcony. To my relief, there wasn't. I congratulated myself on a good job done. I was proud of my timely discovery, alertness, quick thinking and immediate action. Nipped the evil in the bud. Or so I thought!

When I checked again in the evening, my heart sank. I didn't like what I saw. Once again, a whole lot of ants, as if I hadn't cleaned up the night before at all. When I checked, Sonal was not asleep yet. I had to wait until Sonal fell asleep. The wait was torturous. I wanted to make sure she didn't go into the balcony and had to stay in the same room to prevent that from happening. I pretended to work in the balcony so that I would have an excuse to keep the light switched on. When I had to step out of the room for whatever reason, I was hoping she wouldn't find a reason to go into the balcony. She didn't. Crisis averted temporarily. When she slept, the process of the previous night was repeated.

The next morning, she did see a couple of dead ants in the balcony and asked me if what she was seeing were ants. *Merde*! I knew this question would come up sooner or later because even if she knew it was an ant, she would want confirmation from me. I said that it wasn't an ant and that it was a velvet beetle (a fictitious name that I had made up the previous night for such a question), a small insect that looked like an ant. I knew she wouldn't bother to check the internet and would simply believe me. We were safe for some time.

Sure, I lied to her. Tried to pull the wool over her eyes. Strictly, from a therapeutic point of view, what I did was incorrect. As per the requirement of therapy, she is supposed to live with her fears. But I didn't know about it then. Truth be told, even if I did, I doubt if I was going to expose her to so many ants all at once. It would have been insane. She wasn't ready then. She isn't ready even today. So, I lied to her to avoid disaster. For her peace of mind. And ours.

When I mentioned this ants-in-the-balcony episode to my brother on the phone, my brother thought I was beginning to hallucinate myself and asked me if I was actually seeing ants or just imagining them. I can imagine what he must have been thinking. He must have thought I was losing my marbles due to the stress. Which was kind of funny. If it weren't happening to me, I would have laughed. But it was happening to me, and I didn't laugh. I just told him with a great deal of patience (the alternative was exasperation, but it was not his fault to bear my angst) that I didn't imagine it. Not that he could offer me any solutions and not that I expected any from him. It just felt good to unburden myself by venting it out.

I also showed the ants to Shlok one evening. That's the state I was in. I needed reassurance from a six-year-old. He obviously had no wisdom to impart. He looked at me with concern and I told him, I was handling it. I was determined to fight the battle every evening and keep the horrific details from Sonal for as long as I could. *Voyons,* I said to myself!

The next big task was finding a housemaid. If I had to name one person who could make or break the day for Sonal back then and who still can, it would be the humble housemaid. Side note - this is not true only of Sonal, though. As mentioned earlier, in India, almost every household is handicapped without a housemaid. A housemaid is a great leveller in India. Whether you are an engineer, or a doctor, or a high profile executive, there is one person you are forced to bend the knee to - the housemaid.

Since labor is so cheap in India, you could get a housemaid for less than 200 dollars a month. The housemaid would work in your house for 12 hours every day. She would take two leaves in the month. Not even all Sundays. She would dust the house, sweep and swab, clean the bathrooms, do the laundry dishes, and cook for you. It almost sounds exploitative, but it isn't. Because of Sonal's condition, we used to be happy to pay them extra, and the extra was what would come to 193 dollars a month. Hence, a housemaid is one of the most critical components of most family units.

Sonal's life revolves around the housemaid. Nothing could be more calamitous for Sonal than the housemaid taking the day off. Sonal's entire routine goes for a toss. She constantly keeps muttering under her breath or sometimes even loudly enough for me to hear about how disastrous a situation it is that the maid has not come. Thankfully, we found one that suited Sonal. We called for our belongings from Mumbai, and the packers and movers delivered the same. In the next couple of days, the house was fully set up.

When Sonal had finally settled in, and Shlok was also settling down in his new school, Sonal knew that she had dragged her feet enough and that she couldn't put off going to NIMHANS anymore. So, one fine day, when I would not let her put it off any further, we set out to go to NIMHANS.

CHAPTER XXI

The NIMHANS Experience

"*'Hope is the quintessential human delusion, simultaneously the source of your greatest strength and your greatest weakness.' – The Matrix Reloaded*"

We met Dr. Reddy again. We were told about ERP more in detail than we knew until then. Our first visit as a registered patient (as against an OPD patient) - we also got introduced to a young doctor, SM, who was put in charge of Sonal's therapy. SM was a student under Dr. Reddy's tutelage and relatively new to the whole thing. I was a little apprehensive about her skills and about her capabilities. I was hoping Sonal would be put under the care of an expert, but I guess we weren't in a position to dictate terms.

On the positive side, however, since SM was still completing her studies, she was not as hardened and therefore as impersonal as other doctors had been, and that suited Sonal well. Plus, Sonal found it easy to relate to her because she was a woman. So far, so good. SM's cabin was straight out of an old Basu Chatterjee movie with quaint windows, a wooden table, two wooden chairs and a rickety fan. SM seemed eager to make us feel comfortable, and in Sonal's condition, that was a good thing too.

The therapy sessions that Sonal would be doing with her weren't going to be sufficient, and she was told that she would need to practice at home as well. Since she would need somebody to help her with it, I would need to volunteer. That is how I became a co-therapist for Sonal. Here we were finally – face-to-face with ERP.

ERP aims to help the sufferer get used to the obsessive thoughts and make him less likely to engage in compulsive behavior. This is done by helping him confront the stimuli that cause obsessions and resist the urge to carry out the compulsions. So, if a person fears contamination and washes hands excessively as a result, ERP might make him repeatedly touch dirty objects and then encourage him to not wash his hands. I know now that the process works due to the principle of habituation to the task and extinction of the fear. The exposure to the dreaded stimulus repeatedly brings about desensitization to the fear by bringing about habituation to the stimulus.

Undergoing ERP causes great anxiety to the sufferer, and understandably, there is resistance to therapy.

But if done well, this procedure could mean liberation for the sufferer. If done well! That is a big if. To do ERP well, it has to follow a structure. As the first step, the sufferer is made to list all activities or events that act as stimuli that cause anxiety, lead to obsessive thoughts, and force him to do compulsions. All such activities. That could be a long list.

It had close to forty items on Sonal's list. Activities included 'using shampoo', which seemed like sugar syrup to her, 'using detergent' which seemed like sugar to her, 'chocolate wrappers', 'buying vegetables', 'buying fruits', 'going to temples', 'festivals', etc. Most of these activities are everyday activities that I would not even give a second thought to. But they made it to Sonal's list of anxiety-inducing stimuli. Can you now see what she had been reduced to? How badly our routine life was affected? How just getting through the day was an ordeal for her and, as her family, for Shlok and me?

After the list is made, step two in ERP is to grade each of these activities as per their severity. The idea is to sort all these activities into a list that starts with the least anxiety-inducing activity and increasingly goes on to the highest anxiety-inducing activities. One can't just leapfrog to the severest ones without dealing with the simpler ones. That could be potentially disastrous. For Sonal, grading the activities was also difficult because she could not decide between stimuli and grade them differently. After a few false tries, we decided that a work around would be to divide the activities in three clusters, Cluster A containing mild irritants, Cluster B containing average terrorisers and Cluster C containing the real devils.

Step three is to start with the activities listed in Cluster A and achieve mastery over them. In Sonal's case, the least amount of anxiety was supposedly caused by pouring a capful of shampoo on the palm and staying with it.

It was shocking to see just how scared Sonal was of undertaking that activity. She poured the shampoo on her palm but with great hesitation, and it took tremendous willpower for her to keep it on her palm for five minutes before washing it off in disgust. I goaded her to try and keep it for fifteen minutes, but the anxiety was so high that she couldn't. She couldn't make herself believe that it wasn't sweet. This was shampoo which looked and felt like sugar syrup to her and she couldn't bring herself to believe that it was not sweet! This was an activity from Cluster A. Oh boy! Did we have a long way to go or what!

CHAPTER XXII

ERP, Lies And More Lies

"Calvin's Dad: 'The world isn't fair, Calvin'.
Calvin: 'I know Dad, but why isn't it ever unfair in my favour?'
- Calvin and Hobbes by Bill Watterson"

Over the next few days, the same thing continued and also a couple of other activities from Cluster A were taken up. One such activity taken up was keeping a chocolate wrapper (just the wrapper, not even the chocolate) at home on the floor. Earlier she was asked to keep the wrapper in her purse, but the thought troubled her so much that we knew that she wasn't ready for it yet. So, SM suggested that we start with keeping the wrapper on the floor at home first.

Just the fact that we could get chocolates home was a big achievement in itself. That was when Sonal's OCD was at its peak, and we didn't even have sugar at home. There wasn't going to be any sugar at home for a long time to come either. Shlok was to be given Bournvita in milk that did not require sugar. I prefer my coffee without sugar (and I wasn't important anyway), and Sonal would dissolve two Parle-G biscuits in her tea and consume it. So, no sugar. Hence, it was nothing short of a milestone that we could get chocolates at home, even if just for the wrapper. Shlok would gladly wolf down the chocolates, and we would then proceed with the chocolate wrapper exposure.

Sonal managed that beautifully. I was very proud of her. I can't even imagine the struggle it must have been for her to achieve that. To see how much I could push this, one day, I suggested that we keep the wrapper on the floor and go out for a movie. We would dispose the wrapper only when we returned from the movie. I thought Sonal would require some persuasion, but after negligible hesitation, Sonal agreed. That was big, and I was again proud of her. I told her so. She just looked at me and nodded nervously. Sonal didn't freak out even when we returned from the movie, and the chocolate wrapper was lying on the floor. She didn't indulge in multiple compulsions. She merely picked up the wrapper and threw it away. Then she wiped the floor and washed her hands. Done! To expect her to not do even these two compulsions would have been too much.

The basic requirement of ERP is to continue doing all the activities regularly (including those over which control has been achieved). Sonal said that she would do some of the activities herself. One of those activities was the first one she had undertaken, which was the shampoo-on-palm activity. Whenever I would ask her, she would say that she was doing the activity regularly. Initially, I believed her but later, I began to have doubts. The glibness with which she answered in the affirmative made me feel that she was lying to me. Or else, she would have had experiences that she would have wanted to share with me. I wanted to check. So, I marked the level of shampoo in the bottle one day.

The following evening, I asked her if she had done the activity. She said she had. I was crestfallen because the level of shampoo in the bottle had not gone down since the previous day. I assume the same was true for a few days in the past too. I confronted her, but far from being remorseful, she stated belligerently and defiantly that she wasn't doing it and she wouldn't do it because it caused her a lot of anxiety.

I cannot express how miserable a feeling that was on multiple counts. One, my wife was lying to me. Two, she didn't care what I thought about it. Three, the progress that I thought we were making was a chimera. Four, how badly was my wife afflicted for this to cause her enough anxiety for her to lie to me! Not getting better, being found out – neither of these was large enough for her to not yield to her new master – OCD. In her own convoluted way, she believed that she was justified in not doing her exposures.

We took it to SM the next time we visited her. How could I not? I had made up my mind right when the incident happened that I would complain about it to SM because I felt deceived and let down. I had an arbitrator in SM, who I was sure would be able to drill some sense into Sonal. I expected SM to also get angry or at least upset (I don't know why I expected that) but SM was calm about it, and she explained to Sonal like you would to a child that it wasn't good for her to not practice. She told her that the pace could be regulated if it was getting too strenuous for her, but she forbade her to completely give it up. The kind way in which SM explained to Sonal pleased me. I was happy that we had the right therapist finally who would neither be overbearing nor give up.

By now, the medication dosage had been upped, and Sonal was still getting used to it. Psychiatric medication is generally known to have some strong side effects. Plus, Sonal's general health left a lot to be desired, anyway. She had lost close to ten kilos in the past couple of years and was visibly weak, even for routine life. But the kind of life that she had signed up for really took its toll, and the side effects of the medication bothered her even more. She felt drowsy, had no appetite, had an upset stomach, etc. So, she did what a child would. She started skipping medication. I suspected it but had no proof because whenever I would ask her to take her medicines she would say that she would take them later.

One day, when she had her small blue pill in her hand, I was around, and when I asked her to take it, she asked me to go away from the room. I smelt a rat, and while I did leave the room, I kept my ears pinned to the window. Sure enough and I still don't know how, (because we were on the fourth floor), I heard a small sound as if a pebble had been dropped from a height. Believe me, I did. It sounds unbelievable but the truth, as they say, is stranger than fiction. The faint noise was loud enough to make me feel that my world had come crashing down. When I went down with Shlok in the evening, I scanned the place and was not surprised to find what I was looking for. A small blue pill.

Once again, a rap on Sonal's knuckles once again her lies (I dropped it on the floor and hence threw it down, but I took another tablet) and once again admission of guilt after a while. I was so broken I was close to giving up. I told myself that this is not what Shlok and I had sacrificed so much for. This is not what we should be making our son go through. This is not how life should be. Oh, despair, what an abysmal feeling! I was clenching my jaw so hard it began to hurt. Through clenched teeth, I gave her an ultimatum - shape up, or else...Or else, what? I would just have to tolerate this and keep coaxing her. I wrung my hands in frustration, muttered a few abuses under my breath and left the room.

With its ups and downs (more downs than ups), the treatment continued slowly but surely. After a few weeks, SM mentioned that Dr. Reddy wanted to review the progress. Sonal was resentful. She regarded Dr. Reddy like a strict school principal, authoritative and despotic. Come to think of it, I cannot think of a doctor she did not have something against if the doctor was strict with her. Dr. Reddy surely was strict. Not with her directly, but in his overall bearing. Sonal's resentment toward Dr. Reddy was also born out of fear that he might state that not enough improvement was seen or not enough progress was being made.

That is exactly what happened too. While SM, the good-at-heart doctor, continued to be extremely patient with and sympathetic towards Sonal, she came and told us that she was reprimanded by Dr. Reddy after he had seen Sonal. He was not satisfied with where she was at all. He categorically stated that if Sonal wanted to improve, she would have to put in 3-4 hours of therapy every day. This was a gargantuan task for Sonal, considering that she put in only about an hour's worth on her best days and considerably lower on the others. There was indignation at being asked to put in so many hours of therapy every day. There was rebellion. And there were fights. As they say – if I had a penny for every time we fought...

CHAPTER XXIII

The Intensity Of The Problem – Glimpse V

"'The problem isn't the problem. The problem is your attitude about the problem.' - Captain Jack Sparrow"

I had by then begun to resent the ordeal that I was going through. I was experiencing squalor of will; I was ready to give up. In that frame of mind, I used it as an excuse to fight with her that I was strict with her because I cared. My friends (whoever knew about Sonal's condition) lauded my efforts and mentioned that they would have perhaps given up long back. My friends' wives told me that their husbands would have given up on them. Others sympathized with me and expressed wonder about how I was holding up. That stuck, and I started believing that I was doing a lot more than others would have and that my efforts were neither being appreciated nor reciprocated. My constant refrain was that while all I was doing was for Sonal, whatever I expected in return from her wasn't for me. In return for the sacrifices that I was making, all I asked for was that Sonal focussed on her therapy and on getting better. When that was not happening, I used to fight with her. Again, if I had a penny for every time we fought...

Her obsessions were continuing, as were her compulsions. Although some of her compulsions were managed, there were no changes worth writing home about. As a side note, this is what happens during OCD treatment. The sufferer thinks that he or she is putting in as much effort as is humanly possible, but others just don't seem to be able to see it, since there are no radical changes visible. There wasn't too much change in our routine life either. She would still get up stressed and hurry up to finish all her work. She would get up and start crying for no reason. She would constantly be upset and in a foul mood.

After a point, maybe because of the medicines, she would not even get up in the mornings to get Shlok ready for school. That responsibility also landed squarely on my shoulders. Not that it mattered to me because I love the time I get to spend with Shlok, but when we would go down to wait for his school bus, I would be the only father along with 7-8 mothers. While they would be chattering away with one another, I would be standing separately from them, pretending to do something on my phone. It was kind of funny if you ask me now, but back then, I wasn't smiling.

In addition to that, I had personally taken over some of the tasks and was encouraging Sonal's OCD through proxy-compulsion, which is *not* a solution. I was doing it because I was taking much lesser time and doing it with fewer cleaning cloths. If I did it, the tedium of that mundane activity was better than the wastage of time and money if Sonal did it. Not doing it at all was not an option because Sonal hadn't progressed that far. She still hasn't. But to allow her to do it would mean letting her indulge in a compulsion that was bound to give rise to multiple obsessive thoughts and so my doing it seemed like a lesser evil.

Another task I had to take over from Sonal was grocery shopping. Sonal dreaded getting out of the house and shopping for food. Getting groceries would drain her out completely. I knew this was proxy-compulsion too. I had half a mind to refuse to do that but I could either do it or we could go hungry. I had practically no choice in the matter. I had to not only make the purchases, but I also had to check everything to see that there were no ants in any of the packets. One more proxy-compulsion.

Plus, I would have to reassure Sonal that there were no ants. This is a big no-no too. Offering reassurance, I mean. Because, and I learnt this later, offering reassurance amounts to fanning the fire. So, it is to be avoided. But life, as we know, is never lived in black or white. A little tempering is always required. I did not know I was wrong then, but now I do, but I still do it, as and when required. To win a large war by conceding smaller battles.

So, I had to check the groceries. Thoroughly. I had often considered not doing the actual checking and just offering reassurance. Maybe once or twice, I might have done it too. Whenever I did check, I knew at the back of my mind that my checking and Sonal's checking were different. She had developed this hawk-eye vision to spot ants anywhere, and one day what she always feared happened. In a packet of bread, she saw one ant. Oh, the amount of grief I got over it could possibly fill up another chapter in this book. The amount of hysterics that Sonal went through and the tirade she spewed - I was scared she would have a stroke.

I tried to calm her down, but her panic-stricken diktat was loud and clear – get rid of the entire bag with the packet of bread. There was the packet of bread and two packets of tea in the bag. The entire bag had to go, mind you. Not just the bread. I went and gave the bag to a homeless man on the street. I am always hesitant to offer any unsolicited help to anyone, and I wondered how he would react to my offering him food when he hadn't asked for it. I even contemplated throwing the bag away, but I may have a small quirk of my own. I hate to see anything go waste. Taps need to be shut properly, fans need to be switched off when exiting a room, and money and food cannot be wasted. So, I couldn't throw it away, and it had to be given to someone.

Soon, I was rid of the bag, and my next task was to go and manage Sonal. I had to listen to her rants for a good while before she cooled down. But not going home for a while (which I often contemplated but never did) was not an option. Sonal needed to be taken care of. No matter how our relationship was, I felt responsible for her well being and I couldn't ditch her. I know she wouldn't ditch me if the situations were reversed. So, I rushed home for her and for Shlok. I also didn't fancy leaving Shlok alone to cope with the horrors of a hysterical mother all by himself at that tender age.

Sonal would avoid cooking in Bangalore too. Sometimes even for breakfast, we would step out and go to restaurants. Or I would go early in the morning to a restaurant and pick up breakfast for her because she would need tea first thing in the morning, and she didn't want it made at home. Not when she wasn't ready to brave the day yet. Sometimes lunches and almost all dinners were eaten outside. I can scantly remember any instances when we had dinner at home. The waiters at the restaurants also started recognizing us because of our frequent visits. I used to find it awkward. I used to avoid looking at the waiters and acknowledging them. Rather than thinking of my wife's comfort, my shallow mind used to think how wasteful we would be appearing to them eating there every day. I never mentioned it to Sonal then. Nor have I ever, after that.

I implored her often to keep a cook. Maybe cooks in Bangalore would be better than in Mumbai, I said. I reminded her that eating out so often could not be good for Shlok and that he should have as much home-cooked food as possible. I was happy that that got a reaction from her. Realizing the truth in this, she agreed to try out a cook. Sonal met two of them but just couldn't bring herself to hire them. Her reason, as always, stunned me. '*What if the cooks had cooked something sweet in the last house? What if some of the sweet has spilled onto their clothes? What if some of that sweet from their clothes spills in our house? What if there are ants in the house because of that?*'

The perennial series of *what-ifs*. She couldn't muster enough courage to talk herself out of this irrational thought, so we didn't hire any cooks. But we trudged along. She made progress, fell, picked herself up, and moved ahead.

CHAPTER XXIV

An Evening Out With Friends

"'Too many of us are not living our dreams because we are living our fears.' - Les Brown"

To make sure that Sonal had fun without indulging in compulsions and got used to Bangalore life, I also banked upon a few friends that I have there. We would meet them often and socialize together. We would go for movies and dinners. We would go to shopping malls and have Shlok play in the play areas. We would spend the evening in one of their houses and play Uno. Sonal had adjusted well with my friends, and my friends were also aware of her suffering. So, as much as possible, they used to be careful with and around her.

Sure there were misfires like someone ordering for *jalebi*s in her presence and my needing to whisk her away from that place before she got hysterical. Or, she seeing ants in the house of a friend and needing a pill to calm herself down. But by and large, evenings out with friends was something she looked forward to with great anticipation.

It was one such evening when a few of us decided to meet for dinner and go to a restaurant that supposedly served good Punjabi cuisine. We were looking forward to a good time. We reached the restaurant, and my face fell. The restaurant seemed to be a little dingy for Sonal's taste, and since we didn't have a table yet, I thought I should ask her if she was okay with the place. If she weren't, we could have moved off to some other place, rather than waiting.

It had become customary for me to check every restaurant for ants, whether Sonal was with me or not. I remember at least two places that I made mental notes of to not take Sonal to, because of the ants there. It also became normal for me to ask Sonal if a new restaurant that we went to seemed alright to her and whether she would be able to eat there. She would assess the cleanliness and other factors with her in-built OCD microscope and then say yes or no. But she said no, mostly when it was just the three of us and rarely in front of any of our friends, even if she didn't like the restaurant.

In fact, on this occasion, when I asked her if it was alright, she snapped at me for asking her the question. Whoa! Alright, lady! I was both glad and wary that she agreed to eat there just because of our friends. Because I was pretty sure she would have rejected the place had our friends not been there. I however, didn't want to dissuade Sonal from doing something outside her comfort zone. I silently lauded her grit and prayed for the best.

When we were assigned our table, Sonal sat in the corner, and the next instant, as expected, she saw a whole line of ants on the wall right next to her. Within touching distance. She looked so uncomfortable and so out of sorts that I knew that if we didn't get out of the place fast enough, we would have a hysterical human on our hands. Much to the astonishment, nay shock of one of the friends, who wasn't fully aware of Sonal's disorder, we decided to hastily move out of the restaurant. While we were stepping out, Sonal was only semi-conscious and totally unstable – reeling and not even able to stand on her two feet, forget walk. I had to support her lest she fell to the floor. The restaurant owner bewildered though he was, arranged for a chair for her to sit on for a while and also sent a glass of water for her to drink. By now, Sonal had lost complete consciousness.

Curious onlookers looked on, and my confused and dumbfounded friends watched goggle-eyed in a state of absolute perplexity while I sprinkled some of the water on Sonal's face for her to come to. In a few moments, she came to and we decided to head back home because she was in no position to continue socializing. We apologized to our friends for having messed up their plan and having ruined their evening as well. No, no, don't worry about us, they hastily and reassuringly mumbled.

We excused ourselves and came back home, hungry as hell. Sonal decided to sleep her stress away, and Shlok and I stepped down for a bite. He and I went to a restaurant nearby and I coaxed him into having something sweet after the small dinner we had. At least Shlok got to eat something he liked, even though he was hesitating to. Sonal didn't eat anything that evening.

If we went to a coffee shop, the coffee and the sugar sachets could not be taken to Sonal's table. The sight of the sachet opening and sugar pouring out of it into the cup combined with the probability that some of the sugar may remain in the sachet or worse, spill over on the table, would cause her to panic. What I did was order the coffee at the counter, pick up the order at the counter itself (not let the waiter deliver it to our table), put some sugar in the coffee, stir it well right there and give that to Sonal.

Not that it was too big a task for me but what bothered me was that it was too big a task for Sonal. It was a proxy compulsion too. When we were with friends, it was difficult because neither could I have done that for all friends, nor could I have expected everyone to toe the line and pander to Sonal's whims. But I have always had this internal debate. Was I a good husband that I took care of Sonal's comfort so that she experienced little or no stress? Or was I a bad husband for indulging in proxy compulsions just so that my life would be a little more peaceful?

CHAPTER XXV

Exposures In Bangalore

"'As a practitioner of Tai Chi, let me tell you something... Go with a flow of the universe. It is destiny... Forces bigger than us. Don't argue with destiny. It will kick your ass. Believe me.' - Burn Notice (2007 — 2012)"

Once when we were going through her anxiety hierarchy drawn up for therapy, we explained to SM that Sonal was so scared of certain Indian sweets that she wouldn't even dare name them. They were the Voldemorts in her life – they who cannot be named. She used to refer to them by their first letters – G was *gulaab jaamun*, R was *rasgulla,* and J was *jalebi.* SM asked Sonal to utter one of the names. She tried, but she couldn't. So, she refused to. Then as a compromise, SM asked Sonal if she would be comfortable at least writing the names down, even if she couldn't speak them out loud. Sonal thought about this for a couple of seconds, and then, the stress got to her so bad that she fainted. Just the thought of writing down the un-utter-ables made her faint. No matter how many times this happened, I could never get used to it. I would get galvanized into action, trying to find water to splash on her face and bring her back to consciousness.

However, slowly but surely, certain items were being ticked off from Cluster A. Long way to go for Cluster B and even longer for Cluster C. Still, that tiny amount of progress was also welcome. Picking up yet another item from Cluster A, SM once asked Sonal to walk on the grass. This was scary for her because grass could have ants in it and the ants would crawl up her foot and there would be chaos. I said I would help her with it. I kept encouraging her to take the first step. I even did it for her myself (a technique called modelling, where the helper does the activity for the sufferer, models it, so to speak, and the sufferer then draws strength from the helper's action and does it herself) to demonstrate its simplicity and safety.

But she couldn't. She just couldn't. She even tried to take one step and willed herself to keep it on the grass while it hovered in mid-air for ten seconds. But her resolve failed, and she retracted her foot. She gave up. For that day, at least. There was no sense in forcing her to try more, so I let it rest too. When she was making the list of her fears, these seemed weird. But when she was expected to start facing them and could not, the simplicity of the task, combined with the quantum of anxiety that it caused Sonal was bizarre to witness. I just couldn't get used to it. Imagine not being able to keep your foot on the grass. Imagine being scared of that. Wow!

Sonal bravely agreed to go to cake shops and look at cakes as part of her exposure process. Just look at them. Not buy, touch or eat. Just look. I reiterate these seemingly innocuous activities were gut-wrenching for her and to agree to do them took a lot of courage. To go inside a cake shop where there would be other people too watching her squirm or panic, even more so. I wish I had the wisdom to appreciate her act of courage. Since it was normal for me, I took it for granted. There would have been so many such instances where I should have lavished praise on Sonal for her efforts, but I didn't. It was as important for Sonal as it would be for Shlok. She was no better than a small child when it came to therapy.

So, we went to the cake shops. The first time was in a shopping mall. There was a coffee shop that was also selling pastries. We went inside, and she chose to sit at a distance despite a table closer to the display being available. Even physical distance was important. If she sat closer, she would suffer more. So, she sat afar and looked at the cakes and pastries on display for a few minutes. Whatever it was, I was proud of her achievement. This must have been big for her and must have taken a whole lot of courage.

After a short period of time, however, she couldn't bear to look at the cakes anymore and wanted to leave. I didn't want to stress her out anymore than she could tolerate, so we left. I don't know what was going through her brain then. It was fascinating that she and I were looking at the same thing so differently. I was looking at the cakes and thinking how good they looked and wondered if Shlok wanted to eat anything from there. She was looking at them completely differently.

The moment she stepped out of the shop, her knees buckled, and she fainted right there. She may not be getting habituated to her fears, but I seemed to be getting habituated to her fainting. It was unpleasant but not shocking anymore. I was with her, and I caught her before she fell to the floor. Since this was in a busy shopping mall (and in India, shopping malls, with their food courts, play areas for children, affiliations to cinema theatres and loads of window shopping, are synonymous with evenings out) there was no dearth of curious and eager-to-help passersby.

People started gathering around and asked me if we needed help. I politely declined and thanked them for their offer, not wanting to have to explain. Not that I needed help anyway. Sonal is grossly underweight and hence easy to carry. I was embarrassed at the spectacle but also concerned about Sonal. I took her back to the same shop and made her sit in a chair that wasn't facing the cake display. I gave Sonal's purse to Shlok and asked him to pull out Clonazepam from it. He knew exactly what was to be given to mamma, even if he could not read the name on the strip. After taking the pill and having some coffee, she felt better. We hung around for a while until she was strong enough to walk to the car, and then we left.

The second time we did the exposure, it was in a standalone cake shop. We went specifically seeking a cake shop one afternoon and located one a little distance from our house in Koramangala. Since we couldn't just go in and sit there gaping at cakes and pastries, Sonal, with incredible effort on her part, agreed to let me buy a pastry for Shlok. That must have been a herculean task for her, and I thought it was brave of her to agree. Naturally though, he could not eat it on the same table as Sonal. She wasn't *that* strong. At least, not back then. So, Sonal was sitting at one table looking at the display and Shlok was enjoying his windfall at the other table. I had to keep shuttling between the two. Taking care to see that Shlok did not feel alone on the one hand and ensuring that Sonal did not get into a fainting spell again.

But here again, it was a repeat of what had happened in the shopping mall. Watching the cakes for a little while and then fainting. Poor Shlok! He had to ditch eating his pastry mid-way, and we scooted from the shop, thanking the shop-owner, again insisting that we didn't need help. But the fact that she agreed to let me buy a pastry for Shlok was a testament to her efforts, even if we were failing. We were not giving up.

As an aside, I can't sing enough paeans about my car. What a boon it was to have our own transport. I just cannot imagine waiting to hail a cab while Sonal was fainting and having a six-year old along to take care of. Among the unsung heroes that have helped immensely in Sonal's treatment, my car features silently in the list.

As if all that was happening wasn't bad enough, as if life wasn't difficult enough, one day, out of the blue, right outside our apartment window on the floor above, we saw a huge honeycomb. I am not even kidding. A honeycomb that must have been at least a foot long. It had appeared overnight. I was amazed at the speed with which the bees must have built the comb. There may have been no less than a thousand honeybees on it. It scared us all witless. Shlok was scared of the bees' sting. I had mentioned to him that I was stung twice by honeybees as a kid, and it is painful. Since then, he was scared of being stung by a bee.

As for Sonal, she was literally coming apart at the seams. She wasn't scared of the bees, though. She was worried that they were honeybees after all. Because honeybees = honey = sweet = ants. If any of them made their way into our house and spilled the honey they might have on their bodies, there would be ants at home.

How do you like that? I marvelled at the intricate connections she could build from anything at all to ants. All roads led to Rome for her, where Rome = ants. I feared another bout of hysteria from Sonal. So, we had to shut the window. But we obviously could not keep the window shut forever. Regardless of Sonal's apprehension, so many honey bees barely a few metres away were indeed dangerous. Especially, with a small kid at home. The honeycomb had to go.

I went and informed the manager's office about the honeycomb and asked them to get it removed. The person there said they would do something about it, but nothing happened even after 24 hours had elapsed. Every minute seemed risky and no action was taken for 24 hours. Appalling! I reminded them again. Still the same assurances and still no action. I was getting angrier by the day. I finally wrote to the secretary and asked him how much time it would take to mobilize a team that would be able to remove the comb. The garden city that Bangalore is, it would have many such cases, and I was sure there would be people who would be removing these unwanted combs as a business. It enraged me that something so simple should take so much time.

Finally, though, they heeded my frantic appeals and on the third day there was a team that came and removed the comb. It took them three days to bring the honeycomb down, and those three days were the most agonizing days for us. We couldn't keep the windows open, and it would get stuffy. Sonal would constantly glance at the comb apprehensively, and her anxiety levels would shoot up. Shlok would be cowering in terror at the mere mention of needing to open the windows. Unfortunately, it gave rise to another fear in Sonal's mind - the presence of honeybees in and around the complex.

CHAPTER XXVI

Soliloquy

"'I am the master of my fate; I am the captain of my soul.' - Invictus"

Days were passing us by with unnatural speed. Life was strange. Sometimes it seemed to be quite on track. Sonal would be in a good mood, Shlok would be happy, I would be contented. She would do her therapy sessions, we would see some success, which would be encouraging for Sonal. She had started allowing Shlok to go down and play in the complex, including the garden. She herself was walking on the roads again, without letting the sight of sweet or filth bother her too much. She had even started allowing macaroons and sponge cakes to be brought home. This was such an achievement. This was something that we hadn't thought would be possible in a million years. Even SM was happy. She was Sonal's biggest support.

Always encouraging, always available. Kind and compassionate. Shlok was allowed to eat caramel pop corn, which is sweet, and in certain play zones, he would also play a game where he could win chocolates. The only condition was that if he won, he would finish eating all the chocolates before reaching home. Why would a six year-old object to a condition like that? Shlok would be happy. Those few moments are forever etched in my memory as 'happy moments with family'. I was used to waking up every morning and hoping that Sonal's day would be stress-free. More often than not, in the not so distant past, it was but wishful thinking. Now it seemed to be becoming a reality. Winning, I thought, is about the lessons you learn and the personal growth you achieve as you play the game. It's about developing as a person, stretching your abilities and becoming a better you. It means that you will be dramatically different when the game is over than you were when the game began. For now, we seemed to be winning.

In all this, however, I reminisce that I never thanked God. Though it may sound blasphemous, I am not really a staunch believer, and I never remembered to thank Him. I have never been sure of His existence, and at some level, maybe, after so many years of suffering I was tending more towards atheism every day. Or was it spite? I could understand what the Jewish prisoner who wrote, *'If there is a God, he will have to beg my forgiveness'* on the wall of a concentration camp in Auschwitz during the Nazi holocaust was probably going through. Thankfully, my life was far better.

During the epic war of *Mahabharata* when Arjuna was unwilling to fight, because he was standing against his own family, he asks Krishna, *'What is the use of fighting against my own? How can I be happy by slaying my dear ones? They are my uncles and cousins. Won't I be committing a sin? Instead, I would prefer to be killed by them.'* Upon hearing this, the response from Lord Krishna was,

Karmanyevadhikaraste ma phaleshu kadachana.

Ma karamphalaheturbhurma tey sangostvakarmani.

Translated —You have the right to perform your actions, but you are not entitled to the fruits of the actions. Do not let the fruit be the purpose of your actions, and you won't be attached to not doing your duty.

The 16th-century Italian philosopher Giordano Bruno has also said, *'I have fought, that is much, victory is in the hands of fate.'* As much as possible, I try to live by this philosophy too. I try to believe that it is my duty to continue doing my job of tending to Sonal and taking care of Shlok. Whether that leads to success in eliminating her malaise or not is not in my control. I shouldn't let failures deter me or let successes go to my head. I wanted to follow this right through, but it is easier said than done. However, back then, I seemed to be doing an okay job of it. Like Josh Billings has said, *'Be like a postage stamp; stick to something until you get there!'*

So, I stuck

CHAPTER XXVII

The Pressure To Return

"'It is also a victory to know when to retreat.' - Erno Paasilinna"

By this time, it was April of 2011 and we had been in Bangalore for five months already. Pressure had started building from the office, and I knew I would soon have to move back to Mumbai to take charge. For the five months that I did stay in Bangalore, I hardly put in any serious amount of work. My position for those five months was no more than a sinecure. I still asked for another month and made it clear to my boss that if I could not move back to Mumbai in another month's time, I would resign. But I knew I was not in a position to resign because much as they had been abundant when we started off, my financial reserves were fast depleting too. I was too proud to let anyone know about it, but I was at least aware of it myself, and I knew I couldn't go on like that for long. So, it was more bravado on my part than confidence and a faint hope that I would be able to manage moving back and may not have to resign.

The only solace was that Sonal was making progress, and we also knew now how the therapy was to be conducted. I was the co-therapist, and I had taken pains to learn the nuances of the procedure. We had spoken to SM and Dr. Reddy about our move, and they seemed alright with it. That may have been also because doctors hardly ever exert their wills upon their patients. They let them do what the patients choose to do. Dr. Reddy also told us about a therapist in Mumbai, CK, who would continue Sonal's therapy. These small things helped me decide that the time was right to move back to Mumbai. One small niggling thought was that if I had been aware of CK earlier, we may not have had to move to Bangalore, to begin with. I suppose whatever research I conducted in Mumbai to find out if anyone was adept at performing the ERP therapy was not good enough. Anyway, that was over and done with by then, and there was no point in self-castigation.

When I mentioned our returning to Mumbai to Sonal, she was quite upset. She didn't want to move back. She was comfortable with the friends that she had made. She was happy with the clean housing society we were staying in. She had a dependable housemaid. She was happy doing her therapy sessions in Bangalore. She was happy with SM. She was happy with Shlok's school. We had a convivial life in Bangalore, and she didn't miss Mumbai at all. It was ironic that I had to convince her to stay in Bangalore in the beginning, and now I had to convince her to move back to Mumbai. So, I explained to Sonal how my hands were tied and how we had to move back. If I had a choice, I wouldn't have wanted to move back either. I would have stayed back in Bangalore too. But life was handing me lemons right then. I was forced to make lemonade. Withoutsugar at that.

In the same month, which was the last month of Shlok's school and he had his final exams, unfortunately, I had to make a trip to Delhi on work. Getting Sonal's permission to go to Delhi was such an arduous task. Sonal was improving, but she was nowhere near ready to be left alone with a six year-old. She got terribly anxious, and begged me to not go, which soon turned to yelling and a fight ensued again. After a lot of back and forth, when I would not back down, she threw up her hands in despair and grudgingly said '*do what you want*'. I knew I would never hear the end of it, and I was right, but I had no choice in the matter.

Frankly, I also felt that a few days away from Sonal and her disorder would be a breather for me and would enable me to recharge my batteries. A kind of catharsis for my anguished soul, if you may. I would be able to calm myself down and deal with her suffering better. Pity the opportunity came at a time when Shlok had his exams. But I decided to go anyway. So, I did.

While I was away however, there was only one thought in my mind. That nothing untoward should happen back in Bangalore. I had convinced myself that it was too small a window for anything to go wrong since I would be gone just for three days. But it was the first time after almost two years that I was leaving Sonal and Shlok alone and that too in Bangalore, where we didn't have a real support system to talk of. So, I was wary. I had informed my friends and requested them to keep checking, but that was all that I could do.

But those efforts, paltry as they were, were for nought. The worst did happen. Thank you, Murphy! The farther you are from the source of the problem that needs your attention, the worse the problem will be. Worse, it had to happen in the three days out of the five months that I was not with Sonal and Shlok. When I was in Delhi, there was an evening when despite having kept all windows shut (I still puzzle over how it was possible; I feel they may have made a mistake by keeping the windows open), when Sonal and Shlok returned from their evening out, they saw close to about fifty dead or dying honeybees inside the house.

I cannot imagine how scary that must have been for her, considering that I was not there to help either. This caused Sonal to faint with anxiety and Shlok was petrified. I was habituated to her fainting, but not when she was alone with a six year-old, who could barely button his shirt. Imagine such a six year-old all alone at home while his mother is unconscious. That part must have been more traumatizing for Shlok. But I suppose Sonal came to reasonably fast, perhaps subconsciously knowing that Shlok was alone and she needed to take care of him. She willed herself to go through the entire process of getting rid of the dead honeybees and then cleaning the house.

Understandably, it was a mammoth task for Sonal to pick up each honeybee with a paper napkin and throw it away. Once that was achieved, she had to make sure by scanning the entire house that there were no more dead bees left in places where she had failed to check. Then came the task of cleaning up. The whole house was practically washed. The floor, the walls, the furniture, everything was cleaned. Because she couldn't be sure where the bees would have rested their honey-laden bodies and rendered the place sweet. Plus, since she wasn't ever satisfied with one round, she would have done the cleaning more than once. Until she was thoroughly satisfied. All the while, she would have been super-anxious and Shlok would have been terrified. All this, in the middle of Shlok's exams.

After she was done, she was highly strung up. Understandably, she had to vent. So, she called me up and raved and ranted at me for having gone off, leaving them to fend for themselves. Whatever little joy I was feeling of meeting my colleagues again after a forced hiatus of five months dissipated, and I was morose all over again. However, I was as concerned for her well-being and Shlok's as I was upset about my dressing down. At times like these, I could not understand if I was being selfish by seeking some respite from the challenges Sonal's OCD presented or if I deserved the break.

Even when I was to return, I dreaded the thought of facing Sonal. Not only because I would have to listen to her rants again but also because I did feel in the depths of my heart that I had let her down. That it was my responsibility to take care of her and Shlok and I made a mistake. I had placed my convenience over their wellbeing and chose to do what was opportune over what was correct. I did hear a mouthful from both when I reached home. Sonal was stressed and sulky and Shlok was sad and scared. It took me quite a while to calm their frayed nerves down.

By then, I had somehow drilled into Sonal that returning to Mumbai was non-negotiable. We would be returning to Mumbai by the end of the month, and completed the formalities needed for the move. On one of our final few days in Bangalore, Sonal was on the phone with her mother. It has been a big failure of mine that the relationship between Sonal and me was at a point where she distrusted me and rarely shared things with me. In fact, one of my grouses with her was that whenever she skipped therapy sessions or did not follow SM's instructions, she would feel more comfortable in telling SM than she would in telling me. I understand it was largely because I used to get upset at the drop of a hat, and she was scared of talking to me. Even though, on the surface, life was a lot better than it ever was, the communication between my wife and me was still broken, and I could do nothing about it.

On the phone with her mother, Sonal was crying buckets. She would also not let me be in the same room. She asked me to leave. I figured out later that she was telling her mother why she didn't want to leave Bangalore and go back to the same mess it had started from. She was happy in Bangalore. As it is, she was not comfortable with changes in routine, and this was too big a routine to change. So, I remember wishing she was talking to me and not her mother. I remember wondering what we were doing in a relationship where there wasn't enough trust to communicate our innermost feelings. It was sad but undeniable. I knew I had to change the equation. My usual response of being up-in-arms and yelling at her was definitely not the way. This had to be dealt with differently with tender loving and care. I had read the following piece by Brad Pitt, supposedly from Identity magazine, which came to me as a forwarded mail.

(Excerpt begins)

A Secret of Love

My love, who is now my wife, got sick. She was constantly nervous because of problems at work, personal life, her failures and problems with children. She has lost 30 pounds and weigh about 90 pounds in her 35 years. She got very skinny, and was constantly crying. She was not a happy woman. She had suffered from continuing headaches, heart pain and jammed nerves in her back and ribs. She did not sleep well, falling asleep only in the morning and got tired very quickly during the day. Our relationship was on the verge of break up. Her beauty was leaving her somewhere, she had bags under her eyes, she was poking her head, and stopped taking care of herself. She refused to shoot the films and rejected any role. I lost hope and thought that we'll get divorced soon... But then I decided to act on it. After all I've got the most beautiful woman on the earth. She is the ideal of more than half of men and women on earth, and I was the one allowed to fall asleep next to her and to hug her shoulders. I began to pepper her with flowers, kisses and complements. I surprised her and pleased every minute. I gave her lots of gifts and lived just for her. I spoke in public only about her. I incorporated all themes in her direction. I praised her in front of her own and our mutual friends. You won't believe, but she has blossomed. She became even better than before. She gained weight, was no longer nervous and she loved me even more than ever. I had no clue that she CAN love that much.

And then I realized one thing: 'The woman is the reflection of her man'
Brad Pitt

(Excerpt Ends)

I knew it too. I had to just bring myself to do it.

On the last day in Bangalore, as I was handing back the keys to the apartment, I felt that another chapter of my life was coming to an end. I sighed, and not a little sadly, we left for the airport. To go back to our roots. Reluctantly.

The End

CHAPTER XXVIII

Initial Hiccups In Mumbai

"'Sometimes you're the pigeon, sometimes you're the statue.'"

Even the journey back to Mumbai was eventful, but somehow, we made it back despite delays and missed flights. We had decided that Sonal and Shlok would stay in Sonal's parents' house after they landed in Mumbai, and I was to stay at my parents' home. That arrangement was decided upon because Sonal was still scared of living in my parents' apartment and also in the apartment we owned because both these places reminded of her bad days. Not that the days right then were significantly better, but those were worse. So, we decided to stay separately and move in together only when we had taken up a different apartment on rent, and Sonal had cleaned it to her heart's content and made it habitable for herself. Since Shlok's summer vacations were on, having him stay so far away from school was no big deal.

In retrospect, it was amusing, not to mention odd, that we wanted to lease out an apartment to stay in when we owned a perfectly habitable apartment ourselves. We had to tell the broker, who is a friend too, why we were doing something so strange. We intended to give our own apartment off on rent, which meant cooking up a story for the tenants too. Because I doubt if a prospective tenant would understand if I told them that my wife was seeing monsters in our apartment and hence we were giving it out on rent. They'd either consider the place haunted or us crazy. In either case, we would have scared them away. So, we would have to lie. Much ado about nothing, but once again, since Sonal wanted that, that is what we would do if it meant that she'd be slightly happier for that.

So, we spoke to my broker friend and looked for a place while we gave our own place on rent. After we had seen a dozen apartments and rejected all of them, as was the pattern, we finally found one that Sonal was okay with. An exact replica of the one we owned. No change in size, or layout. Same apartment complex. But according to Sonal, it was slightly cleaner. Which made all the difference.

It took over a month for Sonal to set the place in order and for her to feel comfortable enough to finally move there. One full month! During this month, she would travel from Ghatkopar (where her parents stay, which is 17 km one way to the new apartment) everyday, do some work along with her house maid and then go back. But she would have a lot of intrusive thoughts troubling her while there and would not be able to accomplish too much in a day. So, it would take her longer to do routine things than it would take others.

Our apartment had been given on rent too, and the tenant moved in in two days flat. That is how even I would have liked it. Even my parents were beginning to wonder why it took so long to move after the apartment had been decided upon. Just to tell them that Sonal was still getting the apartment cleaned seemed so inadequate and lame. I couldn't get anyone to understand. I am not sure if I understood it myself. The amount of time taken to clean up the apartment was disproportionately huge compared to the size of the apartment. But why was I embarrassed? Why was I not supportive? Why did I have to act like the victim always? I can state confidently that I have done a lot for Sonal and helped her manage her OCD, but I can also state with certainty that I could have done so much better. I just chose to be a martyr back then and make it seem like I was carrying the burden of the world on my shoulders.

On weekends when I wasn't going to the office, she would expect me to be with her. Not that she had anything specific for me to do. She just wanted me around so that I should be available if she wanted something. Or in case something went wrong and she wanted someone to blame. Or, as I explained to a friend that even when she was watching a horror movie, she wanted me to be around - not so that I could fight off the ghost or serial killer in the movie, but for moral support. I was there for a couple of days, but all day, I would sit there just twiddling thumbs. Plus, the house was in complete disarray. Even sitting was a problem. I like my siesta on weekends, which was not possible. I was not even contributing majorly to the setting up effort. I decided that it was a gross waste of my time. So, I refused to follow the directive. There was a barrage of curses and allegations that I was not contributing to the cleaning and setting up. I let her go on with her tirade but did not give in.

In the first week of June, we had still not moved, and from the looks of it, Sonal didn't intend to move anytime soon either. June was when Shlok's school term was beginning. In one of my conversations with her, I was dumbstruck when she said she didn't mind if Shlok missed school for a week or ten days. That was totally unacceptable. So, I told her that if she didn't move by a certain date, I would take Shlok with me so that he could at least go to school. I was made to look like a villain because of that; she went ballistic on me and threatened me with dire consequences if I dared take her son away from her. I inwardly rolled my eyes at the melodrama. She was reacting as if I was snatching her son away from her forever.

In the meantime, I had gone back to Shlok's earlier school and re-secured his admission. True to her promise, the principal just asked me to pay the fees and sent a note to the administrator about Shlok's admission. At least some things were going as per plan.

When we hadn't moved by the weekend before Shlok's school was supposed to start, despite many pleas, I was left with no option other than to go pick him up and have him stay with me until we moved. There was so much drama where I had to explain the logic of my actions to her parents as well, who seemed to have taken it upon them to support their daughter, whether right or wrong. I didn't fault them for taking their daughter's side. They are her parents after all. But even their contention was, '*So what if Shlok misses school for a few days?*'

Huh? I couldn't believe what I was hearing. Shlok was crying because he didn't want to leave his mother. Sonal was crying, alleging melodramatically again that I was separating a child from his mother and that God would punish me and what not. Bulldozing all objections and allegations, I picked up Shlok and headed back to my parents' house. He was crying all the way back, and I had to cajole him and explain why he needed to stay with me for the first few days. He finally relented, maybe out of fear.

I was once again forced to rue the warped life that we were leading, where a child was expected to live away from his mother because she was too tardy to move to a new house quickly because of her OCD. In retrospect, that was one altercation that could have been avoided. Shlok was in the third grade. How much would it have really mattered if he had missed school for ten days? But I was adamant. Perhaps because it was the only way to get her to hurry up with the cleaning and move to the new apartment. Or perhaps, it was my ego.

For the one month that we were back in Mumbai but not staying together, as usual, there was no ERP at all that Sonal did on her own. The road to recovery in OCD is uphill on a slippery slope, and the moment you stop ERP, you start slipping backwards. That is exactly what started happening with Sonal. Some of the progress achieved at Bangalore was once again coming unstuck. I couldn't do much because I wasn't with her. She would tell me off rudely whenever I mentioned it, either using the burden of moving back as an excuse or having snatched Shlok away from her as a counter-argument. So, I bided my time, living with my parents, sending Shlok to school every morning, like a single parent.

A week or so after Shlok's school began we finally moved to the new apartment and started staying together as a family. But there was still no ERP and no mention of it. As is Sonal's wont, (or let me not single her out - as is the wont of people who are expected to make themselves uncomfortable by facing their fears all the time) she kept pushing away the question of reaching out to the new counselor, CK to continue her therapy. All pro-therapy activities with Sonal never got done until she was pushed into it. In matters of therapy, at least, for Sonal, resisting by whatever means possible (*saam, daam, dand bhed* – as Chanakya *neeti* goes) was the default option. If I had not pushed her to fix up an appointment with CK, it might never have happened at all. Or at least, not for a long time. So, I forced her to. Grudgingly and reluctantly, she finally did.

CHAPTER XXIX

The Amazing CK

"*'There is something you must always remember. You are braver than you believe, stronger than you seem, and smarter than you think.' - Winnie the Pooh*"

CK was a practising clinical psychologist at Hinduja Hospital in Mahim. It was a long way off from where we stayed, and we needed to start off well in advance to reach there on time, given the traffic and distance. At least 60-75 minutes earlier. But on the very first day, we left late and reached the clinic late because Sonal was not able to finish her work at home in time. This had become a pattern long ago and it still continued. If the appointment was at 4 PM, she would finish her work and be able to leave only at 3.30 PM. If the appointment was at 5 PM, she would leave only at 4.30 PM. Her work expanded to fit the time she thought she had, and she could never finish her work in time. I would always urge her to leave sooner to reach Mahim on time, but she was never ever able to do so.

She once reached at 5.45 PM for a 5 PM appointment, and CK had refused to see her. In her own distorted worldview, Sonal considered it a slight from CK and held it against her for a long time. She just wasn't able to see where she was going wrong. Everything and everyone had to work their schedules around to fit her lifestyle. I agree that she was perhaps going through more stress than all of us put together. To expect however, that the world would adjust to suit her habits was excessive, but she could not understand that.

Therapy was also supposed to continue at home with me, as per CK's instructions. But, she was just completely powerless to finish her household chores on time and make time for therapy. We had earlier decided that she would finish all her chores by 10.30 PM, and she would sit with me for one hour of therapy after that. 10.30 PM became 11.00 PM, and 11.00 PM became 11.30 PM. Even that was rarely managed. We would manage for a few days, and then, her work would expand to take her beyond the 11.30 PM deadline, and she would not be able to manage therapy. We would often have this conversation,

Me: 'Why don't you ever come for therapy on time?'

She: 'Because I am never sure if I have done my tasks well and feel compelled to do them over and over again.'

Me: 'Sonal, you will need to live with the uncertainty that even if a job is just 70% done, it is a job well done and that you should refrain from repeating the task. Just as in an examination, if you spend a major part of your time doing and redoing just one question, leaving insufficient time for the remaining questions, you may get full marks on that one question but fail the subject overall. Similarly, if you focus on just one task and do it repeatedly just to convince yourself that it has been perfectly done, you will not leave yourself with enough time to do the rest of the work.'

She agreed to work on this, and she did. To some extent, she succeeded too. She made it a point to start therapy at 11.30 PM for a few days after that. But then, as usual, she slipped.

Coming back to CK. CK was a young therapist, and right in the first meeting, she struck me as being sharp and efficient. I was impressed. She quickly assessed what had happened thus far and got right down to therapy. She was already apprised by Dr. Reddy's team and was also in possession of Sonal's Y-BOCS results. She was a no-nonsense therapist with exemplar methods who told me that a lot of stress that Sonal showed was make-believe just so she could escape therapy. She was like a strict school teacher who tolerated absolutely no truant-ism.

On one occasion, when Sonal fainted during therapy, I was going to gently try to make Sonal come to her senses. CK shook her head and gestured to me to not do that. Firmly. She gave Sonal a few seconds and then sharply (not rudely) asked her to get up and told her that she was okay. Sonal got up. Had I been in CK's shoes, I would have told Sonal, *'Okay, don't bother. We shall continue therapy next time.'*

But not CK. The moment Sonal came to, she started off with the therapy right again. CK would also launch into theory whenever a question necessitated it. She was excellent at that too. Never a moment of hesitation. Never a moment of indecision. Always sure of what she was saying and doing. She introduced us to the terms avoidance, proxy-compulsion, reassurance, modelling, egodystonic, egosyntonic and others.

She averred that Sonal was guilty of avoidance. She explained that avoidance was making Sonal's fears larger. The story about Lord Krishna and Balarama illustrates the concept of avoidance well.

Once when Lord Krishna and Balarama were passing through a forest they were tired and wanted to rest. Balarama decided to keep watch and let Lord Krishna sleep first. There came a demon and the demon screamed at Balarama. Balarama, who was shaken up by the scream, shrank in size, and the demon grew larger. The noise woke up Lord Krishna and he saw that there was this large demon in front of him. The demon tried to intimidate even Lord Krishna.

But when the demon screamed at Lord Krishna, Lord Krishna courageously asked the demon what it wanted. No matter how much the demon screamed, Lord Krishna stood his ground. Lord Krishna's courage made him grow larger, and the demon began to shrink in size. Lord Krishna picked up the demon and tied the demon to his *dhoti*. Balarama, astonished to see the demon having shrunk to that size, says, '*When I saw it, it was so big. How has it become so small?*'

And Ved Vyas, through the voice of Krishna says, '*When you avoid what you must face in life, it becomes bigger than you and takes control over you. When you face what you must face, you become bigger than it.*'

It was true of Sonal. It looked like CK was right. Sonal was indeed guilty of avoidance. Hence the problem was becoming so large. We had been accessories to the crime through proxy-compulsion. I was equally culpable for helping Sonal in many ways to get her to complete her rituals, only for the sake of peace.

CHAPTER XXX

The Unravelling

""The greatest mistake is to be continually fearful of making one. A stumble may prevent a fall. To say that we have made a mistake is to say that we are alive. When we cease to make mistakes that is the moment when we cease to be. The Buddha was once asked if he'd ever made a mistake, he answered 'I am making a mistake even now. Nothing more." - Life (2007 — 2009)"

For all her expertise on the subject, CK could not prescribe medication since she was not a doctor. So, she gave us a letter of introduction for VK, a psychiatrist. So, another doctor was added to the list of the countless doctors on whose doors we seemed to be knocking. We visited VK too and ran her through Sonal's entire history, all over again. My first impression of VK was that she had a mature mien with intelligent eyes and a composed outlook. She seemed to be fairly capable too. At least that was a relief. We finally seemed to be meeting the right doctors.

Somewhere, however, at the back of my mind, I had this thought again that had we known about CK and VK before going to Bangalore, we could have probably saved ourselves the trip and the expense and the trouble. I shrugged that thought off immediately. It was a moot point, and maybe, it was necessary for us to go through the entire episode to realize how best to deal with the situation.

Under CK's therapy and VK's medication, Sonal made a lot of progress. But she hated CK. That, to me, was a sure sign that the therapy was working. She always thought that CK and I were in cahoots. That she would chime in with whatever I said, and I with her. That she enjoyed causing her stress. I always had a hard time explaining to her that she (Sonal) and I were not on opposite sides. Neither was CK. Everything was being done to ensure that she got better and for no other reason. As for hating CK, was CK getting any pleasure out of putting Sonal through the gruelling routine? Wasn't it being done in order to help her get better and for no other reason? Wasn't it helping? In her stubbornness, Sonal refused to see reason.

CK was ruthless (and I do not mean it in a bad way) with Sonal and Sonal started feeling constrained. As if her wings were clipped. Outwardly, Sonal would agree to everything CK said. This however, turned out to be a mistake. CK would crack her whip and get Sonal to make a commitment about what she would do and what she would not. Sonal would make promises based on the social desirability principle that is commit on what she thought would be acceptable to CK and not what was within her power to do.

But then, she would decide that she would not be able to follow the strict regimen. She didn't dare tell either CK or me that the prescribed regime was not acceptable to her. So, she would lie - both to me and to CK. When I would catch her in a lie, as usual, we would fight. I would rat on her to CK, who would agree with me, more often than not. Unlike SM, who was kind and non-pressurizing, CK was strict and would tell Sonal when she thought Sonal was slacking off. That is how the thought of me being hand in glove with CK (and vice versa) germinated in Sonal's mind. Pity, there wasn't anything one could do about it.

While there was progress on the one hand where certain compulsions were concerned, Sonal's excessive use of detergents and other cleaning material continued unabated. She would typically end up spending a thousand rupees every week just on cleaning material. That was excessive by any standard. When CK probed that part of her suffering and got that information out, she made Sonal list down item by item everything she was spending so much money on. Then she made her cut it down as much as Sonal was willing to. Unfortunately, like many brilliant ideas, this didn't work with Sonal. CK was doing a fabulous job, and despite Sonal's lying about certain things and running off to her parents when she couldn't cope, she made a lot of progress in other areas.

This listing and cutting down on expenses exposure backfired. Sonal chose to not comply. When this was brought to CK's notice, she warned Sonal that we would have to resort to coercion if she wouldn't follow instructions. She turned to me and rattled off special instructions. One of which was that if there was an excess beyond what was agreed upon, I would have to physically restrain Sonal from performing her rituals. It seemed like an injustice to Sonal, but she was indeed reduced to a state where not exerting force meant allowing her to degenerate further.

So, one morning, when she was spending extra time in the bathroom washing cleaning cloths (by now, there were rashes on her hands due to over exposure to water, and she would flinch every time her hand would come into contact with water and detergent), I asked her to get out of the bathroom. When despite telling her twice, she didn't come out, I opened the door to the bathroom, wrested the soap and cloth out of her hands, physically lifted her, and brought her out amidst her cursing and yelling. I said to her that if she did not listen to me, I would have to lock her up in the room. She cried for a while but finally relented. It would send a shiver down my spine to see Sonal losing her mental faculties in this manner. How would she *ever* get better! I was exhausted.

I would see how she would cringe in pain when she put soap and water on her hands. It would make me cringe to my toes. I vicariously lived her pain. So, I asked her to buy a pair of rubber gloves and wear them when working in water. At least her hands would remain unaffected. Stupid of me because that enables her OCD by allowing her to wash excessively, but I didn't know it back then. I know it now. But it was not a pretty sight to see her struggling in physical discomfort *also*, apart from the mental agony. I got them for her and she tried them for a short time, but couldn't continue with them because her hands would feel hot under the rubber gloves. So, she discarded them as well. Good thing too.

CK would get Sonal to do her therapy using modelling. She would do the exposure herself and get Sonal to follow her actions. She would say, '*See, I'm doing it. Now you do it too.*'

In one of the sessions, CK asked me to get some *pedas*. *Pedas* being a dry sweet, was the right sweet to try out exposure with. She held one *peda* in her hand and got Sonal to hold another in her hand. It was astonishing to see Sonal doing it. She did have a lot of trouble doing it, but she did it. After doing it for a while, CK asked Sonal to keep it, and then Sonal wanted to wash her hands. CK didn't allow her to do it. However, she conceded to let Sonal wipe her hand with a paper napkin. CK asked her to resist the urge to wash her hands until she reached home. Sonal agreed. But then she slyly went to the women's room and washed her hands. But because there was so much that she had done that day, I didn't make an issue out of it and just let it go.

In one of the sessions, CK brought some chocolates. She asked Sonal to hold them. Sonal was able to hold them. Commendable. Then she asked Sonal to put them in her purse. Sonal could not do it. She said she would be able to do it if she were allowed to wrap the chocolates in a paper napkin. CK let her do that and told her that the chocolates would need to remain in the bag until she reached home. Sonal agreed and actually accomplished the task. Little by little, so much progress was being made. It was heartening even though the problem was far from over.

By now, Sonal had agreed to get chocolate chip biscuits and sponge cakes for Shlok at home. That was a considerable achievement. It gave me immense joy to see that the therapy was working and that Sonal was putting in enough effort too. But I had seen it enough number of times to learn that small progress, while laudable, did not mean that we were anywhere close to being out of the woods yet. I had seen more downs than ups. I was both happy and wary of pinning my hopes too high. Fingers crossed!

I had also downloaded a few videos of melting chocolate, and we used to use them for therapy at home. I would show her the videos, and she would try to tolerate the stress that came with it. She managed to expose herself to all types of chocolate ads. True, they caused her great anxiety, but to her credit, she managed that portion of therapy beautifully, and things seemed to be looking up a little. As Paulo Coelho says in The Alchemist, '*When you want something, all the universe conspires in helping you to achieve it.*' The universe did seem to want this to work.

Then one day all hell broke loose. One of the things that CK got Sonal to do at the hospital was to handle flowers. She also used modelling and started off with picking up a flower and asking Sonal to pick one up. Which Sonal did. Bravo! Then CK picked up more and got Sonal to pick up more flowers too. Done. Brilliant! Then CK started stroking her arms, face, and neck with the flower and asked Sonal to do the same. Sonal managed to stroke her arms with the flowers but not her face and neck. Still pretty good. We left the clinic feeling high that Sonal had managed to surmount yet another obstacle with élan.

But doing it at the doctor's once and achieving mastery over it by repeatedly doing it until it causes no more stress are two completely different things. Having done the former is no guarantee that the latter will be done just as easily.

So, we decided to try doing it at home too. We decided that I would get some flowers and help Sonal with the exposure. I would do the modelling, and Sonal would follow suit. Seemed like a workable plan with no foreseeable glitches since it had already been done once. Both Sonal and I were fairly confident that this would work well.

Alas! That was not to be. I got the flowers, and we started off exactly as CK had done. Picking up one flower, getting Sonal to do it and appreciating her effort. Then picking up multiple flowers, getting Sonal to do it and again lauding her progress. Sometimes I think that I don't need a shovel to dig my grave; I was born with it. All hell broke loose when I started stroking my arms with the flowers. Because my flowers behaved themselves but Sonal's flowers (and this has got to be the worst possible thing to have happened to Sonal during therapy), had ants in them, which crawled onto Sonal's forearm. It is difficult to put in words the chaos that ensued at home. First, we were using flowers, which caused stress. Second, ants in the flowers made their way onto Sonal's body. Third, this was not 'under test conditions', in a clinic. This was in the heart of where Sonal is most stressed. Her house.

She cried in horror that there were ants on her body, and repeatedly and vigorously rubbed her arms with a tissue paper to get rid of the ants. Both Shlok and I were frightened about what would happen to Sonal. Then she started screaming at the top of her lungs, started rolling on the floor and crying loudly and uncontrollably. I was terrified to see her in that state. Worse, Shlok was around too, and he was more scared than he would have ever been to see his mother out-of-control like that. He started crying too, unable to control his fear.

With my heart slamming hard against my ribs, I put on a brave face. I hugged both of them, one under each arm, while they cried uncontrollably, trying to soothe their fears down but all the time, shocked and scared, and wondering to myself – what a mess we have gotten into and is there a way out at all or are we doomed to this life of penitence? Penitence for what, again? Would the pall of gloom ever be lifted? Would Sonal ever recover? Would Shlok have a normal childhood ever? Would I be able to wake up someday without having to brace myself for what the day held? Would I ever be able to go to bed at night satisfied that I had a good day? So many questions. No answers.

CHAPTER XXXI

More Bad News

"'The only way to get through it is to get through it!' - New Girl (2011)"

Sonal used to say she could actually see the evil OCD monster in the form of a giant ant - with big eyes and a scary face. It was distressing to see because when I showed her a harmless-looking animation of a friendly-looking ant, she said that that is how the monster looked. I was looking for cartoons of ants so that I could show them to her and she could get used to seeing cartoons first. I had shown it to her on the laptop, thinking that she would be able to tolerate it. Her reaction jarred my senses. She banged the laptop with such vehemence that for a moment, I feared for the safety of the laptop itself. She called the monster a bastard. Sonal does not abuse, and for her to do so meant that her anxiety levels were through the roof.

She stated that the monster appeared whenever she was most stressed or tried to control her compulsions. According to her, it laughed at her otiose efforts to control her compulsions. As if to say, *'You think you are strong? You may succeed for a little while in controlling your compulsions, but let's wait until tomorrow, and we shall see who is stronger.'*

That alone would dampen her already weak fighting spirit, and she would obsequiously give in to her urge to perform her compulsions. She felt that the monster wielded a remote control and she was a puppet that it could control. Or that it used some kind of magic on her. She would feel the equivalent of a physical push to perform her compulsions, and resisting the same not only seemed impossible but would also make her cry all the time for the power that the all-pervasive monster supposedly had on her. She said that she needed to do the compulsions because she was scared of the monster. She would be so scared that she would feel a pain in her chest.

I would hold her close to me despite the fact that there was a distance between us because it was so painful to see her go through this level of terror. At such times, even she would lean into me for whatever comfort I could offer and sob on my shoulder. I would rub her back gently and try to soothe her. I told my friend about it, and looking at the picture of the ant I showed her, he laughed, and I wanted to slap him for being so insensitive. But what would an outsider understand anyway when half of the time even I could not understand? This pain was to be experienced to be understood.

One night after some at-home therapy, which she anyway always did half-heartedly for fear of seeing the monster again, she was terrified and started crying, all the while cowering in fear, her countenance unnaturally pallid, blood completely drained out of her face. Upon probing, she said she could see the OCD monster at home who was laughing at her. I asked her to show it to me. She was afraid of doing it. She said that if she showed me the monster, it would trouble her more. But I insisted, and she pointed to a bare place in the ceiling and said, '*There!*' Of course, there was nothing there. I climbed upon the bed, moved my hand on the spot and said to her, '*See? There's nothing here*'.

She looked at the same spot for a while, looked around and then with confusion writ large over her face, she said, '*It's gone*'. I felt sorry for all of us. For her, because she was going through the terror. For myself, because I was terrified at the nature of her terror. For Shlok, because once again I was apprehensive of the life we were giving him. Made me wonder how many children must be going through a similar fate and I wanted to reach out to them and hug them. I hugged Shlok and pretended I was doing that.

Sonal would sometimes imagine that she could see a line of ants where there wouldn't be any and be really scared and would start crying. I would again have to move my hand over the surface to tell her that they weren't there and try to allay her fears. So, she had started hallucinating, and that was worse than anything we had gone through so far. This was getting out of hand. We needed to deal with this imaginary monster. I was told that seeing a monster is common among OCD sufferers, but for me, this went beyond taking succor from medical theory. My wife was suffering, and she needed to get better. To help her deal with the monster and explain to her how she needed to weaken the monster, I told her once,

'*The obsessions are a way by which your OCD monster, who has gate crashed into your life, tells you that it is hungry. When you perform your compulsions, you are actually feeding it because the monster is bullying you into feeding it. It doesn't care that feeding it troubles you. It doesn't care that the entire process is affecting your daily life, your sanity, your relationships or your happiness. All it cares about is getting fed every time it comes for a visit. It is threatening you that if you don't feed it, if you don't perform your compulsions, it will make your life miserable. It has succeeded in the past in making your life miserable, so you believe what it tells you. You end up feeding it all the time and lose the battle in controlling your compulsions.*

What you don't realize however, is that the reward for your 'good' work in this case is more work. The more you feed the greedy monster, the larger it grows and gets hungry more frequently and consequently, comes to you more often. It has made your mind its bastion because it knows that it has you in its complete control and whenever it forces you to feed it, you will. The monster relies upon the belief that you do not have the strength to resist it even if you want to because you are scared of it, scared of what it can make you do and scared of what it can do to you.

The only way to defeat this wretched monster is to not feed it the next time it makes an appearance and forces you to, by not showing your gullibility and performing the compulsions. It will threaten you if you don't feed it and yell at you, but eventually, if you resist long enough and don't give in, it will go away. It will have to go away.

Or if you cannot resist and do have to give in, at least you will have made an effort to wait for a while and push the monster away. Even if you manage to resist it for a few minutes in the beginning, it would be a step in the right direction, even if you ultimately do give in. And if you are able to resist the monster's bullying altogether, you don't know what you would have achieved.

True, it will return the next time to force you to feed it again, but while he may bully you into believing that it is stronger, it would actually be weaker for not having eaten the previous time. If you persist and do not feed it again, it will go away much sooner this time.

After a few attempts at getting you to feed it, when the monster realizes that it is not going to get its way with you, that you are not going to perform your compulsions, regardless of how much it tries to scare you, the visits will be far infrequent, and soon, it will vanish altogether, and you will be truly free of the monster. Then even if you do see it and it does ask you to feed him, it will be less like a monster and more like a beggar, and you will not only not be scared of it, but you will also be able to resist it without as much as a flutter.

This will cause you great anxiety (far more than you think giving in would cause) in the initial stages when you try to resist the monster, and it seems to return with renewed vigor, but you must realize that it is better to have a festering wound cleaned up and suffer the additional pain that the cleaning up would cause than to let the wound fester and cause septicaemia eventually and risk amputation.'

The rationale is that if, despite performing compulsions, she still continues to remain anxious, is it not better to tolerate some additional anxiety in the beginning in the hope that the anxiety will be manageable or possibly completely eliminated in the future?

She would understand when we talked about it. Still does. She realizes that what I am saying is true. She also realizes that that is the only way to be free of the malaise. But she fails most of the time because when the monster makes its appearance, she loses her nerve and ends up giving in more often than not. Often, she doesn't even make an effort to resist, which causes maximum damage. She realizes that too but is unable to help it.

Sometimes Sonal would crib, '*Why do I have to do therapy? What are the doctors for? Should they not provide me with the medicines to take care of my problem? If I have to do everything myself, why must I go to the doctors at all?*'

I would remind her that medicines only had palliative effects in her case. They may bring about meteoric improvements that are quick and even spectacular but, sadly enough, temporary. A pincer movement attack of both medicines and therapy was essential for a complete recovery. There was no magic wand that could cast a spell to relieve her of her misery. Nor was there any Eternal-Sunshine-of-a-Spotless-Mind type of surgery that would expunge the pain and the memory of it from her brain forever. She would have to find her own mojo, her own anodyne.

When I was in undergraduate college, there was once a small event on Personality Development that I had organized. We had the services of a gentleman named Simon D'Costa who was the speaker. Simon Sir, as we called him then, was a 50 something, semi bald, tall and lanky gentleman. Unassuming and simple. But excellent. Some of what he said still resonates in my mind. When on the topic of 'taking action', he had once said something, which I said to Sonal. I told her,

'*If someone wants to learn football, the coach is available only to instruct, teach the tricks and rules of the game and not to play the game himself. Ultimately, the sportsperson needs to get down on the field and start playing. Not until he starts playing will he be able to master the sport. Unfortunately for you, your suffering is not like a simple headache, which you can get rid of by popping a pain killer. It is rather like a sport, which you will have to keep playing too and best it, whether you like it or not.*

Just as when someone suffers a bone injury, he is recommended physiotherapy in addition to the medication. He cannot afford to not do the physiotherapy if he wants to get well. The physiotherapy may cause him pain, and not doing physiotherapy may offer temporary relief from the pain. But the functionality of the affected part will never completely return. So, in order to get better, he will have to endure the pain caused by the physiotherapy.

The same is true for you too. While you are on medication and while medication seems to be relieving some of the symptoms, if you want to be truly and totally free of your suffering, you will need to endure the pain that comes with the therapy today so that you may have a better tomorrow.

Is it not better to endure some extra pain today and for the duration of your therapy and be completely free in sometime, rather than endure a little less pain lifelong?

Plus, even if you do your compulsions, you are still stressed out. Perhaps more than ever. It is not as if the compulsions relieve your stress for a long time. The compulsions by nature worsen your suffering and make our lives miserable too. Why not give therapy a chance when the upside is complete recovery?'

She would agree when I explained it to her. But was able to do little. She continued to skip therapy continued with her compulsions.

I was happy with CK's efficiency and was confident of her capability in finally delivering Sonal of her woes. At least, to the extent functionality could return to Sonal's life, and by implication, ours too. She was relentless, and her efforts were showing results. She would not stop short at rebuking even me if she thought there was excess on my part. Although we had seen little progress, my hopes had soared. I began to feel that if anyone could make life better for Sonal, it would be CK. But just when it seemed that things would just go from good to better, disaster struck. Disaster for us that is! CK's husband got a transfer to Delhi, and she announced that in a month on the outside, she would be moving. Damn it!

CHAPTER XXXII

The Toll It Took

*"'None of us can choose our destiny and none of us can escape it.' -
The Adventure of Merlin (2008 — 2012)"*

I cannot begin to express what a shock and disappointment that was for me. Here I was hoping that within a few months of therapy, Sonal would be able to live a comfortable (if not completely recovered) life and here was this calamitous news that threatened to topple my castle in the air.

Not that I had a choice. CK suggested that we start visiting a certain TD. TD was a student who had spoken to us to complete some surveys for her final year project when we first went to NIMHANS. She had since then completed her studies and had started practicing. From experts, we were being handed down to amateurs. The disadvantage was that she would be raw and would not have CK's experience. This was a big apprehension. I didn't want some newbie experimenting on Sonal once again. I didn't want the progress undone. Plus, the fact that a change in routine might mean taking a few steps backward, trying to convince Sonal, her dithering, loss of time and what not. The advantage, as pointed out by CK was that she would not come with any baggage and would have theoretical knowledge and concepts fresh in her mind. That seemed like a good reason, but I was still unsure.

Again, not that we had a choice. We had only TD to go to for Sonal's counseling, so I talked her into giving it a shot. As expected there was resistance. It was another change after all. Many arguments and many shouting sprees later, Sonal finally agreed, and we decided to go to TD. But deciding to go to TD and actually fixing up an appointment are two separate things, and it takes a lot of preparation for Sonal to do the latter.

In the meantime, her condition began to deteriorate again. Her existing rituals started worsening, and she had come up with a few new ones too. As may have become evident through these ups and downs Sonal faced, recovery in OCD follows a jagged trajectory. There are several ups but there are an equal number of downs too. Many people do not recover because the improvement seems minuscule to them but the slip backs seem large and disappointing. Sonal was going through it all. Several ups and several downs. It is like a tightrope walk. Right then though, it was more of a down and there was a fear of all progress getting wiped out.

Since Sonal was using biscuits to sweeten her tea, she would need to clean her mouth of any sweetness after she finished drinking it. For that, she would gargle with face-wash. Not toothpaste. Face-wash! Then she would need to wash the tap that she touched with her hands because there could be some biscuit contamination on the tap. Again with face-wash. Lastly, after the entire ritual had been done, she would wash her hands with face-wash. She would thus use up at least two tubes of face-wash on a normal day.

Since we could not keep sugar at home, I suggested once to her that instead of buying sugar, we could buy sugar cubes. They would be easier to handle since you would just need to pick a compact cube and use it. There would be no spilling. She said no straightaway at the mention of sugar. It bothered me that she would not even consider being more flexible. I asked her why and one thing led to another as usual. Fight, fight, fight. It was all we seemed to be doing these days. After major deliberation more suited to international policy making than whether we should keep sugar at home or not, she grudgingly agreed. I was both displeased at the resistance and secretly pleased with the effort that she was making here. I quickly went down to the grocer and bought a packet of sugar cubes.

When I was returning, I was again annoyed (why?) to see that she was standing at the door and had a cloth in her hand. She stopped me at the doorstep. Here we go again, I groaned. She checked the bag to see if there were any grains of sugar on it. Then she took the bag from me as if she was being asked to handle a rattlesnake. She took it to the kitchen where she had spread out newspapers so that if anything spilled, it would spill on the newspaper. Then she dipped her hand into the carry bag and pulled out the packet of sugar cubes. Every deliberate move of her to ensure 'safety' was grating on my nerves as I had pretty much run out of patience by then.

While this process was on, anxiety was oozing out of every pore of her body. She was visibly under tremendous strain. It was sheer will and the desire to do *something*s right that made her undertake this gargantuan task. But naturally, I did not appreciate her efforts back then. What do you think I am? An angel? I was vexingly hurrying her into opening the packet so that we would be done with the elaborate ceremony. She listened to me pushing her for a few seconds and then snapped at me and told me to let her do it at her own pace. I slunk away with my tail between my two hind legs. I knew who the boss was.

No sooner had I turned away than I heard a squeal. Sonal had been holding the packet in one hand and a pair of scissors in the other. When she cut it open, Murphy, who was lurking in the background somewhere, caused one more of his laws to come true. *The more you are careful with something, the bigger mistake you shall make.* The packet almost slipped out of Sonal's hand, and she managed to hold on to it, but one lone sugar cube broke of its prison and spilled out. It fell on the newspaper, yes, but the newspaper was merely a safety net to soften the blow, not a sure shot way to prevent the disaster.

Shlok came running from the room when he heard his mother wailing again. Sonal was visibly shaking because of the acute adrenaline spike and started barking instructions. Get out, she screamed, let me handle this. That instruction was not meant to convey power. It conveyed anguish at having to let her OCD be the master once again, and she, the slave to its bidding. I offered help but was rudely blown off. I failed to see her pain and only saw my own brusies, most of which were to my ego. The larger the ego, the more the bruises and my ego was battered all over. I walked out with a huff and an unkind word, which in her anxiety Sonal didn't give two hoots about.

She shooed me away and began her routine while tears escaped the prison of her eyes. She emerged from the kitchen after a full twenty minutes. Although I was not there, I knew every nook and corner of the kitchen, perhaps even the walls, would have been scrubbed at least twice, if not thrice before her monster master allowed her the satisfaction of feeling that the danger had passed. The sugar cubes had to be discarded. The grocer was surely not going to take an open packet back. We continued to survive without sugar at home.

We used to have an ornate, glass dining table adorning our house. One morning, before going to school, Shlok was sitting at the dining table eating a piece of sponge cake as breakfast. Since he was served breakfast and lunch at school, we did not need to provide him with heavy breakfast in the morning. Sometimes two biscuits, at other times a piece of cake and sometimes half a glass of milk suited him well. This particular morning, it was a piece of sponge cake.

I was reading the newspaper in the bedroom, and Sonal was in the kitchen making breakfast for me. We heard a crack, and then the sound of Shlok crying. Both Sonal and I rushed to see why Shlok was crying. Due to the severe beating that the dining table had taken in its travels (from Mumbai to Bangalore and back) with us across the country, it had weakened and on this day, the glass portion split into two parts. One side of the broken table was on Shlok's lap, and the weight of the table plus the fright of the thing suddenly snapping and falling made Shlok cry. Although the edges were rounded and safe, my first impulse was to lift the glass from Shlok's lap to ensure that it didn't hurt him.

Sadly, Sonal's first impulse was to make sure that the cake he was eating hadn't spilled onto the floor. I didn't know whether to be sad or angry. It was distressing that she rated cleanliness and freedom from ants over Shlok's safety and comfort. It was as if the last vestiges of all goodness and sanity were slowly melting away from Sonal's brain. It wasn't Sonal who had become insensitive. It was her OCD that had made her change her priorities. I know that now. But back then, it seemed to be her callousness to me. Again, after the table had been lifted and Shlok had been pacified and sent to school, I took it up with her and encountered defiance. I guess when I say I took it up, it means I scolded her. By then she had also had enough of my constant nagging and she was more defiant than ever. As always, the situation left me immensely frustrated and angry. At her, at myself, at life in general.

Her rituals were just not abating, and our relationship was steadily going downhill, going through its worst time ever. There was hardly a time when there was any mirth or levity at home. Her problem became so bad that after having prescribed the usual medicines to Sonal for a few weeks, VK also realized the egosyntonic nature of Sonal's problem. Hence, she prescribed anti-psychotic medication to her, to improve her levels of insight. That is a stage where the difference between right and wrong dissipates. She began to feel that her compulsions were correct and what we were saying was incorrect. That was a despairing feeling. From an expectation of 'OCD to better health', we were inching towards a reality of 'OCD with lower than ever insight'.

Every day I would ask her to finish her work in time so that we could sit for therapy, but she just wouldn't be able to. After finishing her daily routine at about 6 PM, she would watch TV for some time. Her favorite soaps would start at 6 PM and get over only by 8.30 PM. I didn't have the heart to expect a compromise from her me-time. So, 150 minutes would be spent unwinding in front of the idiot box. She would start cooking dinner only after that, by about 8.30 PM. She would take 60-90 minutes to finish cooking and serving, and there was rarely an occasion when we would have eaten before 10 PM. By the time we finished eating, it would be 11 PM. After that she would take an hour and a half to wash some vessels, clean the kitchen and take a bath.

She would routinely be free only by 12.30 AM, after which sometimes, she would want to watch some more TV and then would come for therapy only by 1 AM. By then, both she and I would be too overcome by lassitude to even think about therapy. I wasn't sure if she watched the extra TV because she wanted to still unwind or because she wanted to escape therapy. Knowing her state of mind, though, I am putting my money on the latter option.

So, since we were missing therapy everyday with no signs of being able to start anytime soon, with no apparent efforts on her part to chalk out a specific time for it, I asked her one day to think about it and let me know what time would therapy with me suit her. She thought for a bit and said she would be comfortable at 7 PM. Unfortunately, that was not possible for me, with my work hours being the way they were. I told her so. I also felt that she indicated that time because she knew I wouldn't be able to make it at that time. She wasn't the only one with a colored vision there. But I still said I would try to come and added that it would be better if we scheduled therapy closer to bedtime.

The next day I managed my work to be done by 6.30 PM that evening so that I could come home by 7 PM. My fault was that I didn't call her up to tell her that I was coming home earlier than usual and that we could do the therapy as decided. I expected her to be ready for therapy. But she was in the midst of work, and she said she wouldn't be ready by 7 PM. She said I ought to have informed her in advance. I was feeling frustrated for having come home before 7 PM for the therapy, and the therapy was pushed to later. None of our conversations used to be in a civil tone anyway back then. This piece was no different. We were in no time, yelling at each other, without knowing how and without perhaps even wanting to she was adept at nudging the monster in me. The only difference was, back then, I used to think she was the monster. Or her OCD. Not me. Certainly, not me.

Even by 10.30 PM, which was the time she indicated, she was far from ready for therapy. We hadn't even finished eating. The post-dinner cleaning routine was pending too. So, therapy at 10.30 PM was once again pushed to therapy at midnight. I told her that midnight was not a good time for me and while I agreed to do it that day, we would have to find a better time on other days. She countered by saying that she would be able to sit with me only when she had time, and she didn't see how she could manage that at any other time.

To make matters worse, even at midnight, she was still not done with her rituals and by the time she was done, I was asleep. How could I let a chance like that go without creating a fuss about it? We had a huge fight the following morning, as usual. I have begun to wonder if in some perverse, sadistic way, I was also deriving some satisfaction by picking up fights with her all the time. I have to say that I was being pushed into it every time, but you (and I) have only my word for it.

By now, the relationship was shorn of its ribbons and bows and unpacked fully. It had deteriorated so much that we almost couldn't stand each other's presence. Most of our fights would begin because Sonal would refuse to do therapy or, having agreed to do it, not find enough time to do it. Some of our fights were on account of her ever-increasing compulsions, her resistance to accept them as such, and her lying to me to keep them away from me. Some of them were because she expected Shlok to also follow her warped rules, and that would frighten me more than it made me angry because I did not want Shlok to be learning to live a maladaptive life.

Maybe one portion of our fights was because I needed to prove her wrong over and over again. Most of our arguments would be in Shlok's presence. He would watch meekly as his parents went for one another's jugular all the time. Each time I screamed at Sonal or abused her, a part of me inwardly cringed to have Shlok witness all this negativity, anger, and filth. It was just not right for his little brain to absorb all this. But I seemed to be driven automatically, as Sonal seemed to bring out the worst in me. The mood at home would always be black and sombre, and unhealthy.

Sonal's apparent disregard for the compromises on Shlok's part and mine, the inconvenience she was putting us through and unwillingness to follow her therapy regime was the cause of a lot of grief at home. By then, I guess even I was experiencing symptoms of depression because although I didn't go to a psychiatrist for a diagnosis, at least not right then, I used to constantly have an urge to cry and would cry often. Or would be angry and would be yelling at people. Both of which I now know, are symptoms of depression.

VK was consulted, and she asked to see me separately. I was completely tired of the whole affair. The dealing with work, Sonal's disorder, being both the father and the mother to Shlok, and being Sonal's parent rather than spouse, living with so many compromises, constant arguments with

Sonal, no consideration from her for all the sacrifices we were making, no respite in sight had all taken the starch right out of me. I almost said no to visiting her. But meeting VK could be as beneficial to me as it could be for Sonal. So, I agreed. That was another first for me. A visit to a psychiatrist for myself. Me, who was a shoulder for other people to cry on all my life. Me, who solved other people's problems, whether studies related, work-related or personal. Me, who...well! How the mighty had fallen! Superman had met his Kryptonite.

I met VK. It seemed strange to be in her clinic without Sonal. Without being in the caretaker's position but in the care-needer's seat. I had come early and VK still hadn't arrived. As I waited in the lobby of her office, I was replaying these events in my mind and trying to pin down the events that had led me here. But it was impossible to separate the wheat from the chaff. All incidents seemed equally important. Anyway. When I was finally sitting face-to-face with VK, I explained my position to her. She asked me a few questions after we had discussed my situation at length she told me a few things:

I was experiencing burnout. My entire routine included just two things; work and Sonal. So, she said I needed to find some time for myself. Some 'me-time'. To blow away the cob-webs, so to speak. I also didn't realize until VK pointed out that I was having no 'me-time', which was the reason for my irritability and anger. I was focussing all my energies on work during the day and on Sonal and Shlok in the evening and on weekends and holidays. That was a fact. I was an automaton, just intent upon making the day go right. Or, more accurately, not have it go wrong. Wake up, go to work, return, attend to Sonal and Shlok, sleep, repeat. That was how life had become. Mechanical, repetitive and dull.

VK also told me that I was showing signs of depression and that she was worried about me. She suggested that I get on some anti-depression medication. Again, it was a strange feeling for me when I was told I needed medication for depression. All my life, I've had name tags like 'sorted', 'level headed', 'calm-headed', 'shrink' etc. Always happy. Never stressed. Here I was now. Needing medication for depression.

Whatever else I may or may not be, I am a proud person, even vain. I wouldn't be on anti-depressants if I could help it, if there was any other way. I said no to the medication and told VK that I would like to try and beat the depression without medicines first. I asked her whether it could be done. She was also happy that I didn't want to depend upon the medication.

Despite being a doctor, she is the type who chooses to keep her patients off (rather than on) medication for as long as they could handle it. So, she agreed to not insist on medication for me.

But she told me that I was no longer able to do the co-therapists role well. She said that I should recuse myself of the responsibility. Wow, that is a load off! My spirits rose instantly. I was surprised. It seemed like I was submerged underwater all this while, gasping for breath. Being absolved of the responsibility allowed me to rise to the surface and breathe in a delicious lungful of air. What would happen to Sonal was a concern since even though I pushed her the progress was nothing to write home about. And, what if I stopped pushing? But, for that moment, I was feeling mighty relieved.

VK also explained to me that if a child is asked to study all day, the child will never do as he is told and will resent studying. If, however, some time is allocated to studying in a day and it is observed, the child wouldn't mind studying in that allocated time. That is what was happening between Sonal and me. I had taken the role of being a co-therapist way too seriously, and I was pounding at Sonal to do her exposures round the clock. This is why, there was resistance. If we had been able to set a time and do the exposures things could have been different. It made sense, but I let it slide since the monkey of being the co-therapist was going off my back. I wasn't about to ask her for one more chance to do it for Sonal. I was thinking about myself and realized that it was better that I be freed of the burden. I heaved a sigh of relief as I abdicated the responsibility.

For the 'me-time', she recommended that I take up some sport to have adequate physical activity. Or she said that I should start working out. So, I bought a bicycle. Since I had the advantage of working at a distance that could be covered on a bicycle, I used to cycle to work and back. I also used to go to visit VK on my bicycle. That was a good 6 km away from our house (one-way), which pleased VK. Cycling was fun, but I was only doing it for going to the office and back or when I had a chore. If I wanted to do it for leisure, it would mean taking time out and leaving Sonal and Shlok alone at home. That would scare me and also make me feel guilty.

For the 'me-time', VK also suggested that I take up a hobby. I downloaded the Kindle software for my phone, got a few ebooks and started reading. All types of books. Fiction, non-fiction, biographies, anything. I managed to read more on my Kindle in two months than in the last several years. This was done at the end of the day before I slept. Reading on the phone meant that I did not have to keep the lights on and I could do it after Sonal and

Shlok had slept off.

For the 'me-time', VK also recommended that I spend some time with my friends. She said most people manage to make some time for their friends even though they were married and that I needed to do it too. She suggested that I get back in touch with old friends and spend some time with them, which would help me unwind. At one level, it seemed like a selfish thing to do. How could I spend time outside when Sonal and, more importantly, Shlok could need me at home? At another level, I was too tantalized by the thought of some time for myself. I wasn't too much in favor of it, but I also knew it was important. So, I agreed to do that. I then started going out with my friends from work because I was hardly in touch with any non-work friends. Getting back in touch for a reason seemed kind of weird to me. Not to mention, selfish. So, work friends, it was. This meant going out for lunches with them and snatching whatever moments of joy I could with them. Fortunately, despite my changed behavior, some relationships were intact. Those moments with them were some of my happiest moments.

However, when I look back, I realize that I was still not taking time out specifically for myself. I was scrounging it from when I did not need to spend with Sonal. The cycling was for work alone. No jaunts of my own. The reading was after all the tasks of the day were over. I was not making time specifically for the reading during the day. The time with friends was also during work. This made me realize three things. One, I was a slave to Sonal's OCD as much as she was to it. She, however, had only one master, her OCD. I had two, the other one being Sonal herself.

Two, it was not true at all that I did not have time for myself. I just did not know how to make time for myself. Becoming more mindful about the need for self-care helped me make time for my own happiness within the constraints I was placed under. My happiness did not have to mean having to sacrifice Sonal's or Shlok's care. They were independent of one another. All this while, I thought I could have only one or the other. Now I had both.

Three, letting go does not mean failing. Or falling. When I was paragliding in the vacation I talked about earlier, despite being harnessed securely, I was scared of falling for the first few moments. I was holding on to the handle for dear life. My hands were aching, but I believed I would fall if I did not hold on strongly enough. Right then there was an epiphany. Not everyone would have the same strength as I would to be able to hold on the way I was holding on. Also, the makers would not leave it upon the glider to manage not falling off, particularly an amateur.

I felt foolish when I realized this and tentatively let go of the handle. Bracing myself to fall. Naturally, I didn't. Then I let go of my hands altogether and enjoyed the glide. The same was true here. I thought that I had to hold on to the delicate equation for life. That if I let go, we would suffer. That I needed to be in control. But that was proven wrong. I let go of the need for control and survived. Thrived, really.

CHAPTER XXXIII

Getting Worse

But things just went from bad to worse between Sonal and me. I had become increasingly verbally abusive, and Sonal used to hate that. I was not proud of either. I had rarely been abusive with anyone in the past. I had been brought up in an environment where abusing was looked down upon. I didn't like doing it myself. But with Sonal, things had changed. She provoked me so much that it could have been either that or physical abuse. I definitely didn't want to resort to the latter. But my lack of control was something that I was completely ashamed of. Sonal had complained to my father, my brother, VK, and CK in the past. Everyone had brought it up with me. I would resolve to stop abusing, but Sonal would provoke me so much that no matter how hard I tried, I would end up yelling at her, criticizing her, abusing her. Just as mumbling to herself accorded her relief, this yelling and abusing seemed to accord me some relief too. Lalochezia, they call it, the satisfaction one gets by abusing; I was lalochezic.

One day, I pinned her down and spoke to her.

Me: *'Tell me honestly, are you putting in your best effort? You think you can't do any better.'*

She: *'I can.'*

Me: *'This is what I mean when I say that I cannot see the effort. At least, make a beginning somewhere. Make me feel that our efforts are not going waste. Didn't Tolkien, say, 'It's the job that's never started as takes longest to finish?' Make a beginning, somewhere.'*

She: *'Okay. I will try.'*

But then, she never could because of the fear. I used to think she didn't want to.

Sonal had also completely lost any sense of belonging or affection towards either Shlok or me. She would say so. That living with us was nothing less than a burden for her. It would sting back then, and I would think it was terribly selfish of her to make those statements, but I can now understand the how's and why's of that statement. Her suffering was pulling her down, and she was losing the ability to live amicably with us. Every task was related in some way or other to her suffering, and she was feeling burdened by it all. So, when she made that statement, it was emptiness brought by despair rather than a negative feeling towards us. A burden because of the added stress each task was imposing.

But me and my gigantic ego! I would take affront to the slight (as I saw it) and react strongly to it. But why? I didn't seem to have any warm feelings left towards her either. So, why would I expect her to feel warmly towards me? I was the one who was forcing her to do things that she didn't want to do. Shlok had not made any mistakes but needing to take care of him was a task that would take her away from keeping her OCD monster happy. To my mind, she was the monster, not her OCD. I am certain now that in her mind, too, I was the bigger monster. We were monsters for each other. Life sucked.

During that time, I told her one day that if she didn't want to do exposures at home, she could go and stay with her parents. Living with someone who was least bothered about the compromises or sacrifices that the family members had made or the efforts that I had put in was not acceptable to me. To which, she would say, *'What compromises? What sacrifices? What efforts?'*

I would seethe with anger and indignation then and we would end up arguing all over again. That was when Sonal had also started mentioning wanting to get addicted to substances to numb the pain. She asked me, *'Why can't I smoke? Or drink?'*

She never did, though, thankfully. But that was not the worst. She talked about dying as well. She would say that it was better to die than live this life shrouded by misery. She used to say that if she had the courage to commit suicide, she would. It was a dangerous thing to say. Terrorizing. Definitely not something I wanted to leave to chance. I didn't want her to someday end up developing the courage and do something stupid. I didn't want to face a situation where there was even attempted suicide, forget an actual one. Just the thought is giving me goose bumps.

Something needed to be done for Sonal to get out of at least this phase of wanting to end her life. To shake her out of her despondency and nihilism. I let her know that it would be best for her to get admitted to the hospital for some intensive therapy. She resented the idea and defiantly refused. I managed to involve her parents and somehow all of us put together, convinced her. So, I spoke to VK and discussed the situation with her. She was inclined to agree and she said she would write to Dr. Reddy. Her email was:

(Email Begins)

Dear Sir,

After her last follow up at NIMHANS, I have been able to see Sonal fairly regularly. I have done brief marital intervention, and Sonal has also resumed therapy with TD. Overall, there is a good improvement in her approach and understanding of OCD; but symptoms have increased in the last couple of weeks.

She is now willing for inpatient treatment in NIMHANS. I feel that she may be admitted even if her symptoms are of moderate intensity. She has been unwell for quite some time now, and her symptoms are increasing again. So, she will definitely benefit from timely intervention.

Kindly assess her, and consider hospitalisation for intensive therapy.

I will send you a letter with greater details of therapy (done here) with the patient.

With Regards,

VK

(Email ends)

Since she had copied me on the email, and since I thought it didn't cover things well, I added:

(Email begins)

Dear Dr. Reddy,

At home, my experience and discussion with her has been that she doesn't do any therapy beyond what happens at the counselor's office and lately she has started getting suicidal thoughts. She had even considered smoking and drinking in order to relax herself, which thankfully she is not doing yet. She is unable to cope with the pressures of managing the home and the therapy, and my apprehension is that she might try to harm herself.

As a concerned family member, I feel that the situation is more severe than what Dr VK suggests, but of course, that is my personal inadequacy to see what is actually true, which only a trained eye can see. However, this distresses me, and I would like to get her admitted to NIMHANS at the earliest. We have spoken to her about it, and she is ready as well.

Please suggest the next steps to be followed. Is there someone in your team with whom I can speak on the phone and co-ordinate and complete the admission procedure from Mumbai and then get Sonal here, or will we have to come there? Could you also recommend someone whom I can ask questions if I have any because I would not like to bother you for little things?

Do let me know, and thanks in advance.

Regards,

Sunil Punjabi

(Email Ends)

To which Dr. Reddy's response was:

(Email begins)

Unless there is an emergency, month of May is the best time for admission since we are busy with exams in April. For routine therapy related admission, month of May is advisable. Instructions for admissions are available on our OCD website. You have to come here and then make arrangements. Dr (Ms) SM may be contacted for details since she has seen your wife previously.

(Email ends)

So, Sonal decided to wait until May and promised that she would do her best to get better by then.

Before May, however, things started worsening by quantum leaps, as far as our personal equation was concerned. The arguments between us kept getting worse, and the smallest of things became contentious between us. I just didn't know how to get her to agree with anything I had to say. I didn't seem to agree with anything she said either. I could see her withering away, and I believed I knew the answer to her problems. But she didn't believe in them, and she refused to listen to me.

Some years back, one of my friends gave me a beautiful Cross pen as a gift on my birthday. It is one of my favorite possessions, and I use it for whatever little writing I do now. I treasure it and have taken good care of it. Until one day. We had an argument the moment I set foot at home one evening after returning from work, tired and needing to relax. The argument wasn't ending at all and Sonal was becoming increasingly annoying with her whining and complaining. I was so incensed with Sonal that if I didn't take it out on something else, I would end up hitting Sonal. What should bear the brunt of my ire then? My precious pen; I pulled it out of my pocket and flung it hard on the floor, and it split into two. I still have it and it still works, except that it is damaged. My poor pen still bears the scars of my wrath. I walked into the bedroom and banged the door shut, but could not shut Sonal's cursing and screaming down. I was dangerously close to hitting her again, but I had managed to walk out. I was afraid that one of these days I would not be able to stop myself.

On one of the Sundays, I had stepped out for getting a haircut. Hardly had I sat in the barber's chair when Shlok called me up and said that I would have to return home urgently. I dropped the idea of the haircut, apologized to the barber, went back home and found Sonal prostrate on the bed. In great pain. Unable to get up. She expected me to cook for the day because she was not in a position to. She was also irritated about the whole thing. With me, as if it was my fault that she was unwell.

Or maybe, in my colored view, I was seeing it like that because she told me later that it was not like that at all. I didn't believe it, though. Surely, that was not depression. Surely, that was my inability to see how she was suffering, my inability to be empathetic and helpful, and my egoistic need to be considered important, correct and validated. I may be able to see this now. Not then. Then, she was becoming a burden. While she was in pain, I got into an argument with her about the burden it was becoming to manage everything singlehandedly. While she was in pain, she bared her fangs and growled at me. Stalemate as usual. I did what I was asked, albeit unwillingly.

But lately since the burden on me seemed to be increasing and she did not seem to care enough to work on getting better, I just couldn't take it anymore. Which is when I used the D word. I told her that since we were not able to see eye-to-eye when we were living together, it was better if we got divorced. As Yoda from Star Wars says, *'If no mistake have you made, yet losing you are...a different game you should play.'*

I believed I was ready to play a different game.

It wasn't the first time that the word 'divorce' had cropped up in our arguments, but this was the first time when it was uttered and received in all seriousness. At least, uttered in all seriousness by me. What was simmering just below the boil so far had boiled over. She agreed, maybe thinking that it was one of my earlier empty threats, and I told her I was informing my parents. She said okay, once again thinking I would not do it. She did not realize that I was serious about it this time, though. The next moment, I called up my father and told him about the decision. The sacred oath of Omertà was broken.

A few minutes after my phone call with my Dad (or actually while I was on it too), she went red with rage. She asked me,

'Why did you have to take such a hasty step?'

'I asked you and called up daddy only after you agreed.'

'Couldn't you have waited for some time? Why do you have to involve your parents? Did I involve mine?'

'Well, you can involve them now.'

She got hysterical and asked me to get out of the house. It was difficult to contain her. She looked murderous, and I was really scared, not of her, but for her. Daggers in her eyes, she was like a ferocious animal then. She just kept yelling at me to leave and said she would throw my things out of the house if I didn't. I tried to get her to calm down, but she would just not listen. She went on and on and on.

I had had enough too. I wanted to leave too. I decided that I would go and stay over with my parents for some time and initiate the divorce proceedings from there. So, I got up to leave. She was in such frenzy that she said that she didn't want to see my face ever again and that I should leave that very instant. I told her I was leaving and I just needed to get my essential stuff. She wouldn't even give me that much time. I had to beg to be given twenty minutes so that I could pack and leave. There was so much drama over the twenty minutes too. There was continuous opprobrium over my decision for every minute of those twenty minutes. The neighbor came over and tried to pacify both of us. Neither of us was in a mood to relent. I picked up a few clothes and my laptop and made for the door. The neighbor still tried to stop me from going, imploring me not to go. But I knew I was getting out of that place. At least, for that moment.

Shlok was also visibly scared because Sonal was so out of control. He was crying because his parents were not mature enough to manage things amicably. When the moment to decide whether he would stay with his mother or father was upon his head (I hope no child has to ever make that decision), he chose me over Sonal because at least at that moment, I was the calmer of the two, and he was perhaps scared of Sonal right then. This further enraged Sonal, who in her hysterical state felt that she was being deserted, not just by her husband but by her son as well. She passed some nasty comments and made Shlok cry further. She told him that she didn't want to ever see his face again and that he should never ever try to contact her.

Poor Shlok! He was an unwitting party to the madness and definitely did not deserve that. At that point, I figured that taking Shlok away from that house was indeed the best thing to do to keep him inviolate. So, with Sonal crying and yelling in the background, the neighbor looking at us with consternation and Shlok crying too, I left for my parents' house with a few of my belongings, a few of Shlok's, and with Shlok in tow.

A couple of days later, Sonal moved to her mother's house too with our apartment left vacant. I was paying rent but neither of us was occupying it. How ironic! Both Sonal and I had individual keys so we would come as and when we wanted. But even though both of us frequented the apartment for our respective requirements, our timing had never overlapped, and our paths hadn't crossed ever.

But one day, they did. She may have thought I would go to her, and I thought she would come to us. Neither did. Apparently, (this I got to know later), the episode caused her a panic attack and had to be admitted to the hospital for observation. Back then, I thought she was making it up, and I said I didn't care if she was unwell. I was the 'bad guy' right then. Back then, I was always the bad guy. But I was impervious to any insults coming my way from any of them. I couldn't care less.

It was truly the nadir of the relationship. All our altercations notwithstanding, we had continued to be by each other's side in times of need. Here I was now, unconcerned that my wife was in the hospital. Unconcerned about her physical pain, unconcerned about her mental agony. Why shouldn't I be called a monster? I had turned apathetic towards her pain. Apathy genuinely has to be the apogee of hatred.

CHAPTER XXXIV

The Turning Tide

"'Rebuilding relationship requires a lifelong discipline and commitment.' - Sri Amma Bhagwan"

I got a call from VK's clinic. VK asked me to see her urgently. This was uncharacteristic of her as doctors do not generally call up their patients. Obviously, this was something beyond that, and she was concerned about Sonal. She told me that it was time I was put on medication to curb my depression. She said that my efforts were not working, and it was best if I took some medication. I considered what she said. I knew that I was not being able to handle the situation maturely. I knew the extent of anger that I was feeling was wrong. I knew the extent of despair I was feeling was wrong. I was still against the medication, but I knew I could not let my ego stand in the way of my health. So, liked it or didn't, I consented finally.

This was a big downer for me. I cannot emphasize on this enough that I had always been the person my friends used to come to for motivation and for getting their spirits lifted. Hence, when I mentioned to a few of my friends that I was going to be on an anti-depressant, a great many of them just refused to believe me. They had always seen me as someone who would always laugh in the face of adversity and emerge victorious. Even I looked at myself that way. They just couldn't imagine me being on medicines to deal with something called depression. I couldn't either. But there I was. It was time to say goodbye to the image I had about myself. Even when I went to buy the medicines, I was ruing the fact that I was buying medication for myself. Whatever! I had agreed to take them, and I would. But only for as short a period as I needed to. With that thought, I bought the strip.

Coming to terms with my own mental condition was not easy for me. I was resentful for a variety of reasons. I was resentful that Sonal did not work hard enough to beat her OCD. I was resentful that rather than being apologetic, she was defiant about it. I was resentful that all my sacrifices had been summarily dismissed under 'husband's duty' category. I was resentful that even Shlok's wellbeing was not important enough to make her work on her OCD. I was resentful that her parents were not seeing the state that she was in and were enabling her OCD. I was resentful that I was turning into a monster with my anger outbursts. I was resentful that I was turning into a wreck with my crying spells. I was resentful that Shlok was living a sub-optimal life for no fault of his. I was resentful that he was being treated as a piece of furniture in this fracas by both of us. I was resentful that I had to be medicated to manage my emotions.

I expressed all this to VK. She was empathetic but also let me know clearly that I would have to help myself out of it. That if I was going to keep languishing in self-pity, I would stay stuck. That hit me like a ten-tonne truck. Self-pity? But I have the highest degree of respect for VK, and so, I did not lash out at her for being judgmental, cruel and partial. I walked out of her office, promising myself that I would not look for succor here ever again. I would just come for my prescription.

For the first couple of weeks, understandably, there was no improvement to speak of, even after the medicines. Fortunately, though, there were no side effects either. But in those fifteen days, I began to cool down. I do not know whether it was the medicines or effort on my part, (I would immodestly want to claim that it was more the latter than the former) that I started seeing a difference in how I was dealing with situations. I mellowed down. Considerably. I could actually see when I was about to lose my cool, and I was able to prevent it. Kind of like the housefly. Apparently, the housefly's vision is 12 times better than that of humans, and hence when you try to swat a fly, it can escape. It sees your hand coming towards it in slow motion and has enough time to make a clean exit.

Similarly, I could see stress/anger/sorrow coming my way, and I could deflect it in time. Maybe I was becoming more mindful. Maybe it also had something to do with staying away from my source of stress that was Sonal back then. I'm sure it was a mixture of everything put together, not just a singular effort. I asked VK if it was the medicines or my effort. She said it could not be the medicines because medicines took longer. It was more likely my own effort. That pleased me.

However, Sonal and I continued to live separately. I was changing for the better with the others, but I just couldn't bring myself to be civil with her. For the life of me, I couldn't bring myself to agree to go into the hell hole again. I had had more than my share of suffering and felt I was justified in being selfish for once. From Shlok's point of view, I reasoned that there were a lot of children brought up by a single parent who ended up doing extremely well, and so would Shlok. I didn't want him to go through life seeing Sonal and me trying to rip each other's throats out continuously. That, I thought, would be worse for him than living peacefully with one of us. If it meant that I would have to give up Shlok's custody, I would. If it meant that I would have to bring him up all by myself, I most gladly would.

The standoff continued for some more time. We needed to ensure that Shlok didn't suffer. So, we had decided upon a convoluted arrangement whereby he would get to be with both his parents alternately, without Sonal and I having to meet each other. We avoided each other like the plague, and I am ashamed even to relate this incident. It spoke of such a degenerate, lowly existence, not what I wanted for my wife and child in my wildest dreams.

I again wonder who the real monster here was. Sonal's OCD which was making her do all this? Sonal, because she had become so self-centred and vicious? Or me, who should have been more understanding but chose not to be?

But there was a small silver lining to this too. When we started staying separately, Sonal had started becoming an independent person. I always disliked Sonal's dependence and disinterest towards self improvement. But staying separately either gave her enough time to learn, or she realized the need to do it because I wasn't there to do it for her. So, she started learning to do everything on her own.

She took up a teacher's training course to keep herself busy. She also joined a computer academy to upgrade her skills. She bought a laptop for herself. She also started managing her finances herself - doing her own banking and countless other routine chores that had been my responsibility for the time we were together. That was a step in the positive direction. Our communication continued to be sporadic and mainly through text messages. But we no longer stayed frozen in hostility. We were slowly thawing towards one another because the language in the texts had become a notch or two friendlier.

I also had had time to think of VK's stinging allegation about self-pity. Choosing to leave the resentment aside, I approached the topic with curiosity and asked her about it one day. In response, she asked me to read up on cognitive distortions and try to identify some of them in my thoughts. That was VK for you. No ready-to-eat answers. Made you work hard. But Sonal was given homework all the time. So, why shouldn't I be?

I read up on cognitive distortions in Feeling Good, a book by Dr. David Burns. I identified several cognitive distortions that I was a victim of.

Overgeneralization - I had begun to think that all actions of Sonal were wrong without considering other possibilities.

Black or white thinking - I wanted Sonal to be completely compliant, or we would get divorced. There was nothing in between that I could see.

Disqualifying the positive - once again, I realized that I was disregarding all the positive qualities that she had and was focusing only on the negatives.

Mind reading - I was predicting what her responses would be in case I tried to discuss something with her.

Future seeing - To a suggestion about approaching Sonal for something, I was behaving like a soothsayer, predicting Sonal's reactions.

Fairness fallacy - I believed that because I was so good to Sonal (which was also untrue, as I can't say I was good to her), she needed to be good to me too.

Confirmation bias - I was looking for things that were bad about Sonal and finding them.

Magnification - I was blowing things out of proportion. Not all things required the kind of response I was providing to them.

Emotional reasoning - I was not looking at the facts, but at the feelings I had about a situation and pronouncing Sonal guilty.

This is just a partial list. This was unacceptable. I was beginning to realize how large a role I had been playing in the destruction of the relationship.

A month or so later, I fell sick. I ran a high temperature - 104 degrees Fahrenheit - that did not subside even after heavy medication for two days. So, off we went to a specialist at Kokilaben Dhirubhai Ambani Hospital, which is situated close to where we stay. He suggested hospitalization and a few tests, including testing for Dengue. That is what it turned out to be. Dengue fever.

God bless her, for when Sonal heard of it, she came to see me. She would have been aware that she could face censure from my family and me, but still she came. Every day, for as long as I was in the hospital. I am pretty sure she was uncomfortable being there, but she put her personal discomfort aside and did what she thought was right rather than what was inconvenient. That was the difference between us. When it was my turn, I had done the reverse. I may qualify that by saying I was compelled to do it after having given it a good shot, but the fact remains that I had done the reverse. Sonal had the moral high ground here. She also moved back to the house we had rented and took over Shlok's responsibility. She seemed to have mellowed down considerably. Either because she realized that it was best to stay together or because she was being kind to me since I was unwell. Either way, it was obvious that she did not want a divorce and what was uttered was an impulsive mistake.

The evening before I was about to be released from the hospital, she also asked me tentatively,

'Will you come home?'

Meaning would I go and stay with her again. That would have taken a lot of courage to ask. That would have also taken a large heart to at least put behind (if not forgive) the fact that I had been such a terrible husband. Full points to her for that. But I was yet not in a frame of mind to, and I replied in the negative, although gently. She didn't argue, didn't question. She just smiled and said,

'Okay'.

When I was finally ambulatory and discharged from the hospital, my father once sat me down again and told me,

'It is your duty to be completely selfless. Even if she is not doing what she is expected to do and you have to continue to sacrifice your pleasures in order to help her get better, you should.'

'What if she still doesn't understand?'

'Get to that point first where you display complete understanding and don't treat her with rudeness or impoliteness. Where you have stood by her, no matter what. Where you have forsaken all pleasures for her and devoted your life to her betterment. Then you may probably realize that you needn't have thought about separation at all.'

It seemed idealistic to me despite knowing that my father has lived his life pretty much that way and was only preaching what he had always practiced. But can you believe the words? I just couldn't and I was in no mood to relent (despite seeing where I had gone wrong), and take so much suffering upon myself. The life that my father described to me seemed like hell, and I, selfishly, wanted to get out of the mess.

After a few days and after a lot of thought, however, I realized that being selfish wasn't the right thing to do. I remembered the Sioux Indian story of the two wolves, which hit home. The story goes something like this. A grandfather was talking to his grandson about a setback he had experienced.

He says, *'I feel as if I have two wolves fighting in my heart. One is the vengeful, angry, violent one. The other wolf is the loving, compassionate one'.*

'Grandfather, which wolf will win the fight in your heart?' asked his grandson.

The grandfather answered, *'The one I feed.'*

I had to feed the loving and compassionate wolf in my heart. Did I have one? If I did, I would have to revive it first. But I decided to give it a shot because Sonal's coming to the hospital everyday and braving the possibility of being insulted had cracked my cold veneer and the process of a thaw had picked up speed. We were ready to reboot our lives. So, I metaphorically signed the *Sulah Hudaibiya* and moved back in with Sonal and Shlok. With a lot of apprehension, I reached out to VK and asked her to recommend a marital counselor to us for an *entente cordiale*. In the meantime, Sonal had also spoken to her about the same. To put it on a bumper sticker, we shortly found ourselves at the doorstep of RN, a marital counselor.

CHAPTER XXXV

Marital Counseling

"'All relationships go through hell, real relationships get through it.'"

So, we met RN. A smartly dressed, young counselor, who was for the time being practicing in her apartment as her clinic was being set up. The house was on the ground floor and the window opened up to the view of the beach. It was a nice, naturally bright house and RN was courteous and understanding. Being there gave off positivity and it seemed like the right place to be in. The advantage with RN was that she stayed close to where we stayed. So, meeting her first thing in the morning, before going to office was possible. Also, my office knew what was happening and so once a week, when I had to go meet RN, they didn't mind the delay.

I found RN efficient too. Thoroughly proficient in her subject and never unsure of next steps. Whenever we tended to stray away from the topic on hand, she would be able to determine that and bring us back to the topic, rather than get swayed into the story. There were times when Sonal or I digressed into something else while talking about her issues. She had the patience to listen to the rant and the uncanny knack to gently bring the conversation back to the original topic. She wouldn't argue or be as forceful as CK was. Not that the two are comparable, since CK was dealing with Sonal's obstinacy brought about by her OCD and RN was trying to get us to arrive at a compromise through a process of negotiation and conflict resolution.

Even during the marital counseling, in the counseling sessions, Sonal would not be able to distinguish between what was a marital issue and what was an OCD issue. Whenever there was to be any discussion on what problems she was facing with me, her answers would hover around her OCD. RN would try to explain to her why she should restrict herself to marital issues during the counseling sessions by RN. Sonal began to resent RN for that reason.

With RN's help, however, we plodded on trying to achieve some semblance of sanity and order in the deteriorating relationship. Yet again, I'd like to say that I have nothing but the greatest respect for all those doctors, therapists and counselors who, through their knowledge and skills, managed to do such a fabulous job of keeping my relationship with Sonal from breaking. Who at every point in time, motivated Sonal to work towards her recovery and encouraged me to not give up. Because only I know how close I have come so many times to just drop everything and give up.

So often, I have wondered why I am continuing to be in the relationship. Is it because of Shlok? Is it that I do not want to deprive him of the joy of living with both parents? Is it that I think that this life with both parents, no matter how fractured the relationship, is better for him? Or is it that I am continuing because of Sonal? Is it that I feel that without me, who has gone through so much with her and learnt her behavior patterns and the required response to it, she will go from bad to worse? Is it that I feel that she will just not be able to survive without me by her side? In times of self-approbation, I do think that way.

Maybe, in my heart of hearts, I feel that I still haven't given enough to my marriage, and I am capable of giving more in order to make it work. Because I know that Sonal is giving it whatever she can. As they say, just because somebody does not love you the way you want does not mean they don't love you with all they have. Maybe this is the limit for Sonal. Perhaps this is all that she can give. Maybe in her mind, she is giving it everything.

An unhappy young man once went to the old master and said to him that he had had a sad life and he asked the old master for a solution. The old master instructed the unhappy young man to put a handful of salt in a glass of water and then to drink it.

'*How does it taste?*' the master asked.

'*Terrible.*' spat the unhappy apprentice.

The master chuckled and then asked the young man to take another handful of salt and put it in the lake. The two walked in silence to the nearby lake, and when the apprentice swirled his handful of salt into the lake, the old man said,

'*Now drink from the lake.*'

As the water dripped down the young man's chin, the master asked,

'*How does it taste?*'

'*Good!*' remarked the apprentice.

'*Do you taste the salt?*' asked the master.

'*No.*' said the young man.

The master sat beside this troubled young man, took his hands, and said,

'The pain of life is pure salt; no more, no less. The amount of pain in life remains the same, exactly the same. But the amount we taste the 'pain' depends on the container we put it into. So, when you are in pain, the only thing you can do is to enlarge your sense of things. Stop being a glass. Become a lake.'

Stop being a glass. Become a lake. Does it not make it obligatory for me to give it all I have? Or am I so selfish that I will give it only as much as I think I am receiving, even though I can give more and Sonal can't? Questions, questions!

One of my friends asked me a question similar to what my dad had told me. She said, *'Sunil, have you given this marriage all you have? Or will you regret it in the future someday that things could have been better if only you had tried a little more?'*

So, I decided to give it all I had. Because I think I still haven't crossed the Rubicon of tolerance, and I still have a lot to offer to this relationship. I had an assurance from Sonal that she would focus on her therapy and on getting better, and I made promises of not being rude or abusive with Sonal. She promised to go to the doctor and therapist regularly, and I promised to help her as much as I could. We both realized it was a period of great ferment for us, and we decided to play an active role in creating a template of happiness.

Thence started the therapy and the journey, all over again. The Ouroboros had eaten its own tail to sustain its life; in an eternal cycle of renewal, the Phoenix was reborn from its own ashes.

Epilogue

The marital counseling bore fruit. Sonal's efforts at therapy for her OCD showed some more results. Plus, the medication she is on right now keeps her calmer and free of the urge to give in to OCD. At least for the present, life is manageable. She has recovered by almost 90%. The remaining 10% threatens the delicate balance we have managed to achieve, ever so often, but with a few hiccups, we manage. *All's well that ends better*, as JRR Tolkien says. It is better now.

Sonal and I still get into fights. I do not want to leave the impression that I am completely reformed and do not get upset anymore. I still get angry (and so does Sonal), and we still have massive fights. I do not think that will ever end. Not as long as OCD rules the house, at least. Hence, we are always looking for new ways to help Sonal get better. The wrangling between us is not good for us and certainly not good for Shlok. VK had once said to me that Shlok didn't apply to be born to us. We bore him, and it is incumbent on us to give him a good upbringing. Point noted.

This disorder has brought about a silver lining, though. In all this, I realized that I understand counseling. I mean, I really get it. I understand the nuances of dealing with OCD better than most. I decided to pursue it further. I completed my Masters in Clinical Psychology and my doctorate. I completed certificate courses on Cognitive Behavioral Therapy, Neuro-Linguistic Programming, and Life Coaching. I have formed an online support group and now provide one-on-one counseling for OCD. I also launched my own practice - Unshackle Counseling (www.unshackle.in), to provide counseling to whoever needs it, regardless of their capacity to pay. I am in the process of writing a few self-help books to work on living more functionally with different presentations of OCD.

Shlok didn't get a dog. He did not get a baby brother. But we have given him a love-filled life as a complete family unit and not as a fractured one.

True, Sonal hasn't landed a knockout punch to the disorder yet. I guess she never will either. The cure is but a chimera, we know. The Damocles' sword is still hanging over our heads. The climax is yet to unravel, the denouement still light-years away. What will happen remains to be seen. But we are poised to fight this together, and although victory is nowhere on the horizon, we march ahead with one song on our lips – *Que sera sera, whatever will be, will be!*

So, this is our story, ladies and gentlemen.Even if this story doesn't sound like a fairy tale to you, and it did not begin with a *'once upon a time'*, I will make sure that it ends with a *'they lived happily ever after'*.